10/-

5/57

MITHRAISM

SELECT
PASSAGES ILLUSTRATING
MITHRAISM

TRANSLATED, WITH AN INTRODUCTION,
BY THE REV.
A. S. GEDEN, D.D.

LONDON
SOCIETY FOR PROMOTING
CHRISTIAN KNOWLEDGE
NEW YORK AND TORONTO: THE MACMILLAN CO.
Printed in Great Britain
1925

PREFACE

THE Greek and Latin writers of the early Christian centuries make not infrequent reference to Mithraism as a religious and social force within the Roman Empire. Their accounts, however, are neither so full nor so sympathetic as might be desired. The passages here translated are for the most part those published by Cumont in his great work; but for complete understanding they need the illustrations and engravings which his larger book so lavishly provides, and in a less degree the English translation, *Mysteries of Mithra*. The texts, arranged as far as possible in chronological order, are in themselves not always free from difficulty, and in some instances no doubt have been imperfectly copied and transmitted. A few years ago also, A. Dieterich published at Paris and Berlin, in a second edition, *Eine Mithrasliturgie*, with a German translation. There is, however, in reality little, if anything, to connect the so-called " liturgy " with the cult of Mithra, and it did not seem worth while to offer a rendering in English. To a considerable extent it consists of general invocations, magical phrases and words, letters strung together without meaning, relying for their efficacy upon sound not sense, such as are commonly employed in primitive religious incantations. It is possible, though it does not appear probable, that similar recitations were in use in the service of Mithra. They are not confined to any one land or people, but are a universal accompaniment of demonolatry and fetichism.

The brief introduction is intended merely to serve the purpose of elucidating and providing a background for the passages translated. For the early history of Christianity the growth and wide influence of the religions of Asia Minor and of Egypt are of unique importance. Their interaction was far more intimate than is perhaps generally realised. And behind the faiths of the Nearer East lay the great religions of India and more distant Asia, linked by a community of thought and intercourse, the details of which it is probably impossible at this distance of time to unravel. The science and study of comparative religion are only at the beginning of the service which they are able to render to the religious thought and sympathy and intelligence of mankind.

A. S. GEDEN.

Harpenden,
October, 1924.

MITHRAISM

INTRODUCTION

THE most serious rival of Christianity within the Roman Empire in the early centuries of our era was Mithraism, the worship of the deathless and glorified Sun. Less extravagant than most of the cults which, from the nearer East, had flooded Rome with strange gods and stranger rites, it made like them a strong emotional appeal to the worshipper. And the more sober and thoughtful elements of Roman society found in its teaching present consolation in trouble, and an assurance of a bright future beyond the narrowly drawn limits of this life. Doctrines of a similar character were professed and taught in most, if not in all of the Eastern faiths that had migrated to the West; and it was this responsiveness to the longing of the human heart which gave them such power and permanence as they possessed over and above the gorgeous and attractive ritual which they set up. Christianity sympathized with these truths, and in purer form enforced them in her teaching and had made them an essential part of her creed. Widely divergent therefore as were the faith and worship of the Christ from the Mithraic cult, there underlay the rites and ceremonies of the latter, which to us often appear uncouth and grotesque, a doctrine and truth which was illuminative and uplifting.

And it was this element which gave to the creed its persuasive and enduring power.

To the student of history, however, it appears strange that in the literary sources of the early Christian centuries, and in the writings of Christian apologists and commentators, references to Mithraism are comparatively few, and there seems to be inadequate recognition of the serious menace which its extension and popularity offered to the supremacy of the Christian faith. In view of the very large number of Mithraic sanctuaries which are known to have existed within the Roman Empire, it is hardly possible to interpret this silence in the sense that the menace was not so real as it appears to us to have been, or the rivalry so acute. The latter is probably true; partly for the reason that Christianity was, and had been since the days of the Apostle Paul, a religion of the cities. It found its strength in the population of the townships, in Rome itself, in the capital cities of Greece and France, of Africa and of the Provinces generally. Mithraism was the religion of the army and followed the troops in the garrison towns and the great cantonments on the borders of the Empire. The officers and soldiers were its supporters, and into the circles in which the Christian propaganda so successfully wrought the faith of Mithra made little attempt apparently to enter. The contact between the two religions was therefore, at least in the earlier period, not so intimate as has sometimes been represented, and the opportunities of mutual interference or conflict were rare. The Christian thinkers and apologists cannot have been ignorant of the powerful hold which Mithraism had established within the Empire. They do not seem, however, to have recognised fully the danger to which their own position and claims were exposed by its attractiveness and success. Until with the accession of the Emperor Julian (360 A.D.) there came a brief era of reaction, and for a time Mithra was triumphant.

Ethically and religiously the strong attraction which Mithraism, in common with other cults of the Orient, exercised on the peoples of the Roman Empire was due essentially to two elements upon which their thought and teaching laid stress. It was not all pomp and rhetoric, strange rite and elaborate symbolism. An attempt at least was made to respond to the craving of the human heart for rest from the consciousness of sin, and to unfold a reasonable and reasoned doctrine of a life beyond the grave. The official Roman paganism had no assurance to give in regard to these great matters of capital importance as far as the ordinary citizen was concerned, however true it might be that the Emperor, even before his death, was enrolled in the pantheon of the unageing gods. Mithraism offered to its votaries a way to the forgiveness of sins, by which the consciousness of guilt might be removed, the sting of remorse drawn, and the peace and joy of innocence regained. And in all its symbolism and teaching it assumed and emphasized the continuity of life through and beyond death. To the devout Mithraist death did not end all, in a blank wall of ignorance and night. He was offered a sure hope of resurrection. As the grain of wheat renewed its life in the dark ground, and blossomed forth into the living ear; and as Mithra himself, the lord of light, issued forth each morning to recommence a glorious life which the deadening shades of night had only interrupted not destroyed; so for the believer, the initiate, there was the assurance that death was not the final issue of life, that the revival which nature everywhere experienced was a promise and pledge of his own, and in the confidence that he would live again he might take comfort.

That these doctrines and the ritual forms in which they found expression were not without their effect, probably unconscious, upon the teaching and language of some at least of the later Christian apologists and teachers may be regarded as established. It is possible, on the other hand, although perhaps not likely, that Christian ideas and sentiments made their way into the Mithraic cult, and were adopted in Mithraic rites. With all that they held in common, however, the creeds were yet essentially independent and distinct; the debt on either side, if debt there were, was in form and detail only; and morally the superiority of the Christian teaching was great and incontestable. According to some writers also there are references to Mithraic doctrine in the Epistles of St. Paul and in the Apocalypse. It is not impossible that this should be so. The evidence, however, is inconclusive and is differently interpreted. St. Paul himself in later life, or the author of the Revelation, may have come into contact with Mithraism, and have been impressed by the dangers to which the Church was exposed by its insidious teaching. Other Oriental cults, however, were at least as active and prominent within the Roman Empire in the first century of our era; and their relations to one another and to Christian teaching are not a little obscure.

Name and Origin.—Like the faith itself the name of Mithra is of Oriental origin. In the ancient sacred books of India and of Iran, Mithra (Mitra) is the sun, deified and reverenced, and a solar cult under this name would seem to have been part of the joint religious heritage which the two great nations or families of nations carried with them from their ancient home.

In India the name, though not the cult, was early superseded by other and more popular forms of the sun-god.
It was otherwise in Persia and the nearer East. It is
true that in the Gāthās, the oldest metrical portions of
the Avesta, the name does not occur—perhaps inten-
tionally removed—but in the later parts of the sacred
books it becomes increasingly prominent, and there
are some indications that Mithra occupied in ancient
times a position of supremacy, a " father of gods and
men," to whom all other deities were subordinated.
As early as the fourteenth century B.C. his name is
found with those of three Aryan deities in an inscription
from Boghaz Keui recording a treaty between the ruler
of Mitanni and the Hittite king, and from this it is
inferred that the service of these gods was carried on in
the latter kingdom. Later in the Zarathushtrian reform
or revival, which had for its object the exaltation of
Ahuramazda, the claims and rights of Mithra were set
aside, and instead of occupying the first place, holding
the scales evenly between the rival subordinate powers
of good and evil, he is relegated to an entirely lower
position, as one of the creations of Ahuramazda. Indications, however, remain in the texts of his former
greatness; he is the first of the *yazatas*, sustainer and
defender of the truth, guardian and guide of the righteous
dead, rendering effective aid to Ahuramazda in his
combats with the demons, and is invoked in prayer.
In later dedications and inscriptions he is the divine
giver of victory.

It would seem, therefore, that in the broader accepta-
tion of the terms neither the time nor the place of the
beginnings of Mithraism can be definitely ascertained.
The worship of the sun-god probably originated indepen-
dently on the sun-lit plains of Central Iran, as in India

and other parts of the ancient world. It may, however, have been due to a foreign source, established and developed elsewhere, and carried by early settlers to the favourable environment of Bactria, modern Persia and the adjacent countries. In these lands the religion of Mithra, if not indigenous, was established at a very early date, and the material is wanting for a reconstruction of its antecedent history. The primitive migrations of peoples are only less uncertain than the faiths they bore with them. Some figures on early Persian monuments with a circle of rays around the head, traditionally supposed to represent the prophet Zarathushtra, have been claimed for Mithra himself, but there is no real basis for the conjecture. " Mitra " or " Mithra " signifies " associate," " friend," and it was in the kindly aspect of the god that the worship of the sun found a congenial home and place of nurture for many centuries in ancient Iran.

In such an environment, however, it was impossible that the faith should remain uncontaminated and alone. From all sides other cults and other deities, most if not all of them crude and naturalistic, were pressing for recognition. An early illustration of this syncretistic tendency is perhaps to be found in the intrusion of the Aryan gods, above noticed. The native beliefs and superstitions also, animistic and magical, varying in name and form and ritual in every district, were a constant source of danger to its purity as soon as ever Mithraism moved from its early home. The reform of Zarathushtra was essentially an endeavour to expel the foreign and unworthy elements, as he conceived them to be, from his native faith, and to restore and maintain its primitive truth and simplicity. The name " Mithraism " in the narrower and more technical meaning is of course of much later origin and application. The continuity of the faith, however, was maintained from very early times. " Mithraism " served itself heir to a long ancestral line, the beginnings of which are beyond the recorded dawn of history. But the accretions that have been gathered in during a long history are of great variety and number, and it is not always practicable to indicate the source whence they were derived. Kindred beliefs and philosophies, primitive superstitions and magic, abstract speculation, nature-worship and folk-lore, have all made their contribution to a rich and varied whole, in which these elements have more or less readily combined.

Diffusion.—Mithraism therefore by origin and birth-place was a faith and cult of the Nearer East, and was only one, although perhaps the most important of the Oriental religions which permeated Rome and the Empire during the early centuries of the Christian era. Within the Empire's limits Mithraism appears to have been practically confined before the beginning of our era to Asia Minor, where it had adopted native rites and found itself at home among native modes of thought. Its eclectic and syncretistic spirit would seem to have facilitated its extension among peoples of a religious temperament, but with no systematised creed or cult. The opportunity for its rapid movement toward the West was given by the methods and requirements of the Roman military system. The agents responsible for this diffusion of Mithraic thought and worship were mainly two : the soldiers recruited for the Roman armies from among the warlike tribes of the nearer East, who carried with them to the most distant military camps their faith and ritual and proselytizing zeal, and seem to have proved themselves untiring and successful

missionaries of the religion of Mithra; and to a much
less extent, perhaps with less opportunity, captives from
across the border sold as slaves in the wealthy house-
holds of the Roman cities or of the great landed pro-
prietors, who in their new homes maintained their
religious beliefs and taught and practised their accustomed ritual. The military colonies also were centres
of Mithraic light and leading.

Moreover the principal trade-routes were arteries
along which Mithraic ideas found their way to the
West. The agents in this diffusion were similarly
Eastern merchants, who carried with them their own
faith and religious rites, and together with settlements
for trade and commerce established in the various
countries the worship of their own deities, and made the
provision necessary for the maintenance of religious
custom and ritual. How far definite attempts at
proselytism were carried forward in these new centres
it is not easy to determine. Probably the attractiveness of the new faith with its promises of release and of
hope for the future proved sufficiently powerful to win
disciples in at least as great numbers as the newly-
founded communities were able to assimilate, without
any strenuous efforts at propaganda or expansion;
and these converts were drawn from all strata of the
population, not only from the lowliest and the poor,
but from the wealthy nobles, the Roman knights, and
the highest in the land. In all probability, however,
the greater number of the votaries of Mithra belonged
to the lower classes. In definitely Greek lands the
appeal seems to have met with comparatively little
success. Few traces of Mithraic worship have been
found in Greece proper. To Greek philosophy and
thought the problems of regeneration and the future

life, of which Mithraism professed to offer a solution, were not new; and the answers which their thinkers had worked out through the centuries, if somewhat bewildering in their variety, were more acceptable than the speculations of a foreign creed.

If the sites upon which Mithraic sanctuaries or monuments have been discovered are plotted upon a map of Europe and the Nearer East, as is done for example in the map published in Cumont's *Textes et Monuments* or the English translation *Mysteries of Mithra*, they will be seen to extend from the extreme borders of the Roman Empire in the East to the British Isles in the West, but on the frontier of the Empire from the Black to the North Seas they are especially numerous. The provinces of Dacia, Pannonia, Noricum, and Germania are rich in remains of the faith of Mithra. The Roman garrisons along the Scotch border line also have left traces of the presence of the cult. In the neighbourhood of Rome and in North Italy sculptures and monuments of Mithraic origin are widely diffused, but they are found more rarely in the South of France, and a few only have been discovered in Spain. In Asia Minor itself they are not numerous, and in North Africa they are rare, nor does the faith seem to have penetrated into the interior. A solitary monument has been traced at Memphis, and there was a sanctuary and worship at Alexandria. A Mithræum existed also in London.

The total number of the monuments it is hardly possible to estimate. In some instances the Mithraic character of the remains is uncertain. Several hundred, however, are known, dating from the middle of the first century. With the collapse of Julian's power in the year 363 A.D. and the restoration of Christianity Mithraism appears to have lost its hold and gradually decayed. No

precise date, however, can be assigned for its final
disappearance.

Sanctuaries.—The Chapels or Sanctuaries of Mithraic
worship, as they are known from existing remains or
from the accounts of contemporary writers, are apparently modelled in regard to their form and situation
upon the ancient primitive rituals of Phrygia and Asia
Minor, celebrated in the open air or in the dens and caves
of the mountains. Without exception as far as is known
the sanctuaries were of small size, capable of accommo-
dating only a limited number of worshippers or of
candidates for initiation. They were crypts or caverns
either wholly artificial or artificially enlarged, and in the
cities at least for the most part underground, in dark
caves or cellars from which the natural light must have
been almost altogether excluded. Several of these
small *Mithræa*, or sanctuaries for the celebration of the
mysteries, are found within a single city such as Ostia
or Rome, and they give the impression both of exclusive-
ness and of a cult discountenanced, and perhaps harassed
by the prevailing religious authorities. The larger
chapels consist of a nave or fore-court, beyond which
was a smaller chamber leading to the actual crypt or
sanctuary, approached by a few steps, in which the
celebration of the sacred mysteries took place. At the
back of the crypt was a relief or sculptured scene of
Mithra in the act of slaying the bull, with other animal
figures symbolic of the facts or truths presented in the
mysteries. Statues or figures also of Mithra himself
and of his attendant torch-bearers were placed sometimes in the crypt or the anterior chambers, and by the
side of the main altar stood a font for the holy water of
purification. Along the sides of the chamber were stone
benches, or a raised daïs, on which probably the cele-

brants took their places at the ritual of service. One of
the most elaborate and complete of these Mithræa has
been found on the military frontier at Carnuntum on
the Danube, near Vienna. In addition to the ordinary
sculptures it contained two altars, of different sizes, and
a stone lion, the emblem of strength and lordship,
sacred to Mithra.

The sculptures found in London are described by
Cumont, Vol. II. p. 389 ff. and reproduced from photo-
graphs. They were discovered in the City in or near
Walbrook during some excavations, and according to
Cumont's statement are preserved in a private museum
at Hitchin. The Mithræum probably stood therefore
not far from the present site of the Bank of England.
The inscription on the chief sculpture states that it was
dedicated by a certain Ulpius Silvanus, a soldier of the
Second Augustan legion. The sculptures themselves
are supposed from their style and the marble of which
they are composed to have been brought into London
from abroad. Monuments also of Mithraic origin have
been found in York and Chester, as well as on the
frontier in Scotland, as would naturally be expected in
centres of military importance.

Symbolism and Worship.—Of the details of the ritual
and ceremonies observed in these sanctuaries of the
Mithraic faith little is known. Derived as they were
for the most part from the native rites and worship of
Asia Minor, they would not be lacking in scenery and
pomp designed to impress the eye and captivate the
senses of the worshipper. In the darkness or semi-
darkness of the caverns and underground chapels, the
shrine itself, in which the principal ceremonies took
place, would be illuminated with artificial light to
throw into relief both the symbolic sculptures at the

B

further end of the shrine and the figures of the officiating
priests in their rich vestments celebrating the mysteries.
The scenic effects were no doubt designed especially to
impress the candidates for initiation; a world of light
and forms of suggestive symbolism and spiritual interpretation were opened up before them, whereby their
mind and thought, already dazed perhaps by the
brilliancy of the illumination and the novelty of the
worship, might be led away from earthly things, and
concentrated on the mysteries and hopes of the world
to come. As enumerated by Jerome (*infra* p. 61),
there were seven grades of initiation through which the
neophyte passed, as he became fitted to receive higher
teaching and to enter into fuller communion with the
Divine. There were grades also of priests, modelled
upon the Zoroastrian priesthood in Persia, and the
most influential positions and rank appear always to
have been in the hands of an elect few, to whom were
confided the secrets of the highest knowledge beyond
the reach or the capacity of the ordinary worshipper.
As the figure of Mithra himself, so the entire ceremonial
and symbolism were Oriental in their presentation and
character.

It is unfortunate that the extant accounts of Mithraic
customs and worship are for the most part from unfriendly
critics, whose purpose was not to exhibit the best or to
offer a fair and complete exposition of a faith and worship
with which they were out of sympathy and of the real
meaning and intention of which they had little understanding, but to select what of barbaric observance or
complex doctrine appeared to them capable of easy
ridicule or of effective denunciation. The monuments
themselves are dumb; and their significance or place in
religious thought can only be inferred from the literary

references, and from the analogy of other faiths and legends. The brief dedicatory inscriptions in their stiff and formal phraseology give no information upon the spirit in which the worshipper approached the shrine, or the truths which he believed to be there presented. Though domiciled in the West, Mithraic ritual and thought remained true to its Eastern source, and appears to have undergone little change or modification during the centuries of its life in the cities and military camps of the Roman Empire.

The central figure in the sculptured relief which forms the background of the Mithraic shrine is always the tauroctonous Mithra, the god bestriding the bull and in the act of slaying it by thrusting a sword or dagger into its neck. This supreme divinity Mithra is himself an example of the syncretism, through and in which the faith took its rise. The ancient Iranian god of light was identified with Shamash, the Babylonian sun-god, and Mithraism adopted and assimilated many of the beliefs, legends and traditions which had held sway on the plains of Babylonia from a greater or less antiquity. As god of light, and ruler of the upper air, Mithra was mediator or intermediary ($\mu\epsilon\sigma\iota\tau\eta s$) between the gods who inhabited the upper world and the lower world of men ; and according to one form of the legend, soon after his birth from Chronos or Time he entered into conflict with Shamash, whom he vanquished and bound to himself in a perpetual covenant of friendship and alliance. He is represented in many sculptures as born from a rock ($\pi\epsilon\tau\rho\omicron\gamma\epsilon\nu\eta s$ or $\pi\epsilon\tau\rho\eta\gamma\epsilon\nu\eta s$) and is worshipped by shepherds who had witnessed his miraculous birth. The bull was the first and noblest, apart from man, of the creations of Ahuramazda, and Mithra for some reason which the legends do not explain was commanded to slay it.

With his dog he pursued and caught the bull, dragging it on his shoulders to the cave, where it was put to death. Mithra was therefore taurophorous (ταυροφόρος) as well as tauroktonous (ταυροκτόνος). From the dying bull issued the seed of life to the world. And thus the act of Mithra became the sign or symbol of regeneration, from death to life, and the worshipper at the shrine had perpetually before his eyes the reminder that death did not end all, but was the gateway to renewed life. The spirit or soul of the bull was received into Heaven, and there deified as the guardian of cattle.

The significance or symbolism of the other figures of the sculptures is not altogether easy to interpret, nor are the extant accounts of much assistance. An apology or explanation from a votary of Mithra, if such had been preserved, would have made much plain that at present is obscure. Accompanying the central figure of the god himself are usually two standing figures, one on either side, bearing each a torch in the right hand, whence their name " torch-bearers " (δᾳδοφόροι, δᾳδοῦχοι), the one upright, the other inverted and pointing downwards. They have been explained, not very convincingly, as duplicates of Mithra himself, or as representing the rising and the setting sun. It is probable that they symbolised in some way the light and heat of the sun, as inseparable attributes of the god. It is natural to compare the two youthful attendants on the Buddha, that appear on the Gāndhāra sculptures. These also have been interpreted as replicas of the Buddha. Whether there is any connection between the scenes from the East and the West is uncertain. Possibly a common origin should be attributed to them.

Around and beneath the central figures of Mithra and the bull are grouped other figures, the significance of which is more or less apparent. The ears of corn express the renewal of life in an ever-changing, ever-recurrent cycle. The scorpion and the serpent typify the forces of evil, that endeavour to neutralise and destroy the regenerative power derived from the life and death of the bull. The bull itself was no doubt considered a symbol of the strongest natural vigour and energy. The dog of Mithra watches the scene. And in the canopy of the heaven above are set the signs of the zodiac, or the sun and moon. In this last symbolism the influence of Babylonian astrology is evident. In the sculptures much was due also to Greek art, and the face and figure of the victorious god, as he consummates the death of the bull, bear a strong resemblance to the representations of the youthful Hercules. The legends of the sufferings and exploits of the god also are clearly borrowed from or modelled upon the traditions of the Greek hero. Other stories have their origin in Jewish sources, and reproduce with more or less closeness and fidelity the narratives of the Pentateuch. To relieve the sufferings of mankind in a great drought, for which the powers of evil are responsible, Mithra shoots an arrow into the rock, and water immediately springs forth. Similarly in a deluge of water covering the earth one man is warned and saves himself with his cattle in a ship. These and other scenes are variously represented in the sculptures.

Mithraism therefore made its appeal effective, in great part at least within military circles, but also to the downtrodden and enslaved, to whom it offered the prospect of freedom and the amelioration of their lot in a future life. The traditions concerning the god exalted the military virtues of courage and endurance, and represented the triumph through conflict of strength enlisted on behalf of right and justice against violence and wrong. How far the cosmology and the legends were accepted as a matter of faith it is impossible to determine. But the popularity and success of the religion of Mithra did not depend upon the stories of its origin. To the wistful outlook into the future it gave a clear and prompt response; and in so far as its foundations were laid upon a real human longing and need, it was secure of a ready acceptance. Even the Christian propaganda does not seem to offer an adequate or equal parallel to the wide and rapid extension of the faith of Mithra. It was unable to avail itself, as did Muhammadanism, of the power of the sword. But in the declaration of the forgiveness of sins and the purification of the wrong-doer from his guilt, and in the doctrine of a new life, a life renewed and perpetuated through death, Mithraism found a spiritual strength which carried it far and wide, and which seems to have won for it the enthusiastic support and devotion of its adherents.

Decay and Disappearance.—The causes of the decay and apparently rapid decline of the influence and popularity of the Mithraic cult are obscure. Undoubtedly its decline went to a not inconsiderable extent hand in hand with that of Rome's military power. But the zenith of its greatness and prestige appears to have been passed before the Roman legions, especially as recruited from the provinces of the Near East, retreated from their outposts on the frontier. Undoubtedly the criticism and opposition of Christianity had something, perhaps much to do with its declension and ultimate eclipse. From the Mithraic point of view it was unfortunate that the features of ritual and symbolism which lent themselves to misrepresentation and abuse were more prominent than the esoteric doctrines which appealed to the inner circle of more thoughtful disciples and initiates. Of this the Christian polemic did not fail to take full advantage. It is fair also to remember that our knowledge of these ceremonies and of the beliefs they represented is derived mainly from the narratives of opponents, whose prejudice and interest, to say the least, were not enlisted on the side of presenting Mithraic cult and faith in their most favourable light. Mithraism failed before the rivalry of a dominant and more aggressive faith which wielded the powers both of an established religion and of eloquent schools of teaching and defence, but also before the winning and persuasive force of the larger truth. And it was well for the world that it failed. The period from the middle of the first to the end of the third century may be regarded as the time when Mithraism reached the highest point of prosperity and influence. Thenceforward it appears to have gradually lost its hold, and to have ceased to be of real consequence among the religions of the Empire. Probably it lingered long in obscure districts in the provinces, and among the more tenacious and conservative elements of the military party. Of the details and stages however of its decay nothing is really known.

Literature.—It would serve no useful purpose to give a long list of references to Mithraism in published works. The standard authorities are the publications of M. Cumont, mentioned below; next to these perhaps in interest and importance are the articles in the encyclopædias, summarising knowledge on the subject. It would not be difficult to extend the list. In all the works named, however, there will be found much that is of great value, contributing to a real understanding of the

conditions of the world and of the social and religious
life in which the religion of Mithra found itself.

F. CUMONT, *Textes et Monuments figurés relatifs aux
    Mystères de Mithra*, 2 vols., Brussels, 1899; " The
    Mysteries of Mithra," translated from the second
    revised French edition by T. J. McCORMACK,
    London and Chicago, 1903.

S. DILL, *Roman Society from Nero to Marcus Aurelius*,
    London, 1904, ch. vi, " The Religion of Mithra ";
    Roman Society in the Last Century of the Western
    Empire, 2nd ed. *ibid.* 1899.

J. TOUTAIN, *Les Cultes Paiens dans l'Empire Romain*,
    Paris, 1911, ch. iv, Le Culte de Mithra.

W. WARDE FOWLER, *Religious Experience of the Roman
    People*, London, 1911.

T. R. GLOVER, *Conflict of Religions in the Early Roman
    Empire*, 3rd ed., London, 1909, especially in relation
    to *Plutarch*, p. 105, *Justin*, p. 191, *Lucian*, p. 210,
    Celsus, p. 256, *Tertullian*, p. 317 f.

L. PATTERSON, *Mithraism and Christianity*, Cambridge,
    1921.

A. DIETERICH, *Eine Mithrasliturgie*, 2nd ed., Paris and
    Berlin, 1910.

A. V. WILLIAMS JACKSON, *Zoroaster, the Prophet of
    Ancient Iran*, New York and London, 1901; Persia,
    Past and Present, *ibid.*, 1906.

Arts. " Mithra, Mithraism," in Hastings' *Encyclopædia
    of Religion and Ethics*, vol. viii, with the literature
    there cited, in the *Encyclopædia Britannica*, etc.

AVESTA

Mithra in the Avesta.—The passages in which Mithra is referred to in the Avesta are numerous, for his worship was of great antiquity and importance. A selection of them only can be given here. Antedating, as they do, by many centuries the rise of Mithraism in the later and more technical meaning of the term, they illustrate and define the character of the god who held the supreme position in this later cult. From early times the sun was almost universally an object of reverence, and already in the Avesta the deification of the visible solar orb has been effected and the attributes of his person determined and described. In this respect the *Mihir Yasht* is of especial importance and interest, being occupied entirely with the praise of Mithra, invocations and prayers to him for help, and descriptions of his offices and character. As the deity of light he sees and knows all, visits upon the wrongdoer his sin, and as an impartial judge renders to every man according to his deserts. In the pantheon of Iran he holds a similar position to that of Varuṇa in the Rig-Veda. The renderings are from *S.B.E.* vols. 23, 31.

> *Sîrôzah* II. 16 : We sacrifice unto Mithra, the lord of wide pastures, who has a thousand ears and ten thousand eyes, a God invoked by his own name.

With slight variations the same words are elsewhere more than once repeated.

19

Fravardîn Yasht I. 18 : The man who in life shall treat the Fravashis of the faithful well will become a ruler of the country with full power and a chief most strong. So shall any man of you become, who shall treat Mithra well, the lord of wide pastures.

Zamyâd Yasht VII. 35 : Then Mithra seized that glory, Mithra, the lord of wide pastures, whose ear is quick to hear, who has a thousand senses. We sacrifice unto Mithra, the lord of all countries, whom Ahura Mazda has created the most glorious of all the gods in the heavens.

Mithra, therefore, is a creation of Ahura Mazda.

Vîshtâsp Yasht I. 4 : Mayest thou (Vîshtâspa) be freed from sickness and death like Peshôtanu (son of V.). Mayest thou have piercing rays like Mithra. Mayest thou be warm like the moon. Mayest thou be resplendent like fire.

Mihir Nyâyish : We sacrifice unto Mithra, the lord of wide pastures, who is truth-speaking, a chief in assemblies, with a thousand ears, well-shapen, with ten thousand eyes, high, with full knowledge, strong, sleepless, and ever awake.

We sacrifice unto Mithra, the lord of all countries, whom Ahura Mazda made the most glorious of all the heavenly gods. So may Mithra and Ahura, the two great gods, come to us for help (*i.e.* to give help). We sacrifice unto the undying, shining, swift-horsed sun.

*   *   *   *   *   *

We sacrifice unto Mithra and Ahura, the two great imperishable holy gods; and unto the stars and the moon and the sun with the trees that yield baresma. We sacrifice unto Mithra, the lord of all countries.

Mihir Yasht I. 1, 4 f. : Ahura Mazda spake unto Spitama Zarathushtra saying : Verily, when I created Mithra, the lord of wide pastures, O Spitama, I created him as worthy of sacrifice, as worthy of prayer as myself, Ahura Mazda.

*   *   *   *   *   *

For his brightness and glory I will offer unto him a sacrifice worth being heard, unto Mithra, the lord of wide pastures.

We offer up libations unto Mithra, the lord of wide pastures, who gives a happy dwelling and a good dwelling to the Aryan nations.

May he come to us for help. May he come to us for ease. May he come to us for joy. May he come to us for mercy. May he come to us for health. May he come to us for victory. May he come to us for good conscience. May he come to us for bliss. He, the awful and overpowering, worthy of sacrifice and prayer, not to be deceived anywhere in the whole of the material world, Mithra, the lord of wide pastures.

Ib. II. 9 : On whichever side he has been worshipped first in the fullness of faith of a devoted heart, to that side turns Mithra, the lord of wide pastures, with the fiend-smiting wind, with the cursing thought of the wise.

Ib. V. 17 ff. : Unto whom no one must lie, neither the master of a house, nor the lord of a borough, nor the lord of a town, nor the lord of a province.

*   *   *   *   *   *

On whatever side there is one who has lied unto Mithra, on that side Mithra stands forth, angry and offended, and his wrath is slow to relent.

Ib. XIII. 56 ff. : With a sacrifice in which thou art

invoked by thy own name, with the proper words will
I offer thee libations, O most beneficent Mithra.

*   *   *   *   *   *

Listen unto our sacrifice, O Mithra. Be thou
pleased with our sacrifice, O Mithra. Come and sit
at our sacrifice. Accept our libations. Accept
them as they have been consecrated. Gather them
together with love, and lay them in the Garônmâna.[1]

Grant us these boons which we beg of thee, O
powerful god, in accordance with the words of revelation, riches strength and victory, good conscience
and bliss, good fame and a good soul, wisdom and
the knowledge that gives happiness, the victorious
strength given by Ahura.

Ib. XXIV. 95 : Who goes over the earth, all her
breadth over, after the setting of the sun, touches
both ends of this wide round earth, whose ends lie
afar, and surveys everything that is between the earth
and the heavens.

Ib. XXVII. 106 f. : Should the evil thoughts of
the earthly man be a hundred times worse, they would
not rise so high as the good thoughts of the heavenly
Mithra.

The same formula is then repeated in succession for
" evil words," " evil deeds."

*   *   *   *   *   *

Should the heavenly wisdom in the earthly man be a
hundred times greater, it would not rise so high as
the heavenly wisdom in the heavenly Mithra.

And thus, should the ears of the earthly man hear
a hundred times better, he would not hear so well as
the heavenly Mithra, whose ear hears well, who has
a thousand senses, and sees every man that tells a lie.

[1] The Paradise of Ahura Mazda.

Yasna I. 11 : I announce and complete (my Yasna)
to the two, to Ahura and to Mithra, the lofty and the
everlasting and the holy, and to all the stars which
are Spenta Mainyu's creatures, . . . and to the
resplendent Sun, him of the rapid steeds, the eye of
Ahura Mazda, and to Mithra the province-ruler.

Ib. II. 11 : In this Zaothra with this Baresman I
desire to approach Ahura and Mithra with my praise,
the lofty, eternal, and the holy two ; and I desire to
approach the stars, moon and sun with the Baresman
plants and with my praise, and with them Mithra
the governor of all the provinces, and Ahura Mazda
the radiant and glorious, and the good heroic bountiful
Fravashis of the saints.

Gâh Hâvan 2 : To Mithra of the wide pastures,
of the thousand ears, of the myriad eyes, the Yazad
of the spoken name, be sacrifice, homage, propitiation,
and praise.

Mishna 'Abodā Zārā, II. 3 : The following articles of
the heathen are prohibited, and in such wise that no
benefit may be derived from them : wine . . . and
skins with an incision at the animal's heart—Rabban
Shim'on ben Gamliel says, " only if the incision is
circular, but not when it is made lengthwise."

The passage is not improbably supposed to refer to the
sacrifice of the bull in the Mithraic cults.   The Talmudic
comment or explanation of the judgement quoted from
Gamaliel is to the effect that a circular form of the skin
around the wound indicates that the latter was inflicted
before death ; if the animal was dead when the wound
was inflicted the skin did not contract but remained
straight.   There is no reference to Jewish ceremonial

slaughter.[1] The 'Abodā Zārā, " strange service,"
" idolatry " is the eighth treatise of the fourth book of
the Mishna, סֵדֶר גְּזִיקִין, book of " Damages," and treats of
the relation of the Jews to idolaters and their practices.
Like the rest of the Mishna the date of the treatise cannot
be exactly determined. It contains older and more
recent elements. Traditionally the final settlement and
revision of the whole work was due to Rabbi Yehuda
ha-Nasi, Judah the Prince, towards the end of the second
century.

> *Herodotus :* Others are accustomed to ascend the
> hill-tops and sacrifice to Zeus, the name they give
> to the whole expanse of the heavens. Sacrifice is
> offered also to the sun and moon, to the earth and
> fire and water and the winds. These alone are from
> ancient times the objects of their worship, but they
> have adopted also the practice of sacrifice to Urania,
> which they have learned from the Assyrians and
> Arabians. The Assyrians give to Aphrodite the name
> Mylitta, the Arabians Alilat and the Persians Mitra.

Herodotus of Halicarnassus on the south-west coast of
Asia Minor was born towards the beginning of the fifth
century B.C., and is believed to have lived to the age of
about sixty years. The " Father of History " based his
narrative upon written and oral information accumu-
lated during extensive travels in Egypt and elsewhere;
and the doubts at one time widely felt and expressed with
regard to his good faith and accuracy have been almost
altogether refuted. His great work appears to have
occupied him until his death, and he died leaving it

[1] See W. A. L. Elmslie, *The Mishna on Idolatry*, p. 31, to whom
I am indebted for note and rendering; cp. also *ib.* p. 20.

unfinished. The reference to Mithra is found in the 131st chapter of the first Book. If the text is correct Herodotus has been misled in regard to the identification of Mitra or Mithra wth Aphrodite. Mithra was a male, not a female divinity.

Ktesias : Ktesias reports that among the Indians it was not lawful for the king to drink to excess. Among the Persians however the king was permitted to be intoxicated on the one day on which sacrifice was offered to Mithra.

The text is derived from the encyclopædic work of Athenæus of Naucratis, who lived at Rome towards the end of the second century of our era, wherein are preserved quotations from many ancient writers, not a few of whom would be otherwise unknown or unrecorded. Ktesias himself was a Greek of Cnidus in Caria, a younger contemporary of Herodotus, who practised medicine for many years in Persia under Artaxerxes Mnemon, and wrote a history of Persia in twenty-three books down to the year 398 B.C., which is now known only in the quotations of later writers.

Xenophon : (*a*) Do you wonder at this, Lysander? I swear to you by Mithra that whenever I am in health I never break my fast without perspiring.
(*b*) By Mithra I could not come to you yesterday without fighting my way through many foes.

The words of the first passage quoted are put into the mouth of Cyrus the Younger, addressed to Lysander, *Œconomicus,* IV. 24. The latter citation is from the *Cyropædia* VII. 5, spoken by Artabazus to Cyrus the Elder. In either case little more is indicated than that

the oath by the god was a popular form of speech,
regarded as of more or less binding force.

>   *Duris :* In the seventh book of his *Histories* Duris
> has preserved the following account on this subject.
> Only at the festival celebrated by the Persians in
> honour of Mithra does the Persian king become
> drunken and dance after the Persian manner. On
> this day throughout Asia all abstain from the dance.
> For the Persians are taught both horsemanship and
> dancing; and they believe that the practice of these
> rhythmical movements strengthens and disciplines
> the body.

The quotation is due to the same source, and reports
the same custom as that of Ktesias above. If the report is
correct, or true at least of the period at which the writers
lived, the king was under a *tabu* to refrain from wine,
which *tabu* might be broken on the day of the Mithraic
festival; and apparently according to Duris his subjects
place themselves for the time being under a compensa-
tory *tabu*. The statement does not seem to be corrobo-
rated by other writers. Duris of Samos was born about
the middle of the fourth century B.C., and his " His-
tories " covered a period of nearly a century, beginning
with 370 B.C. Fragments only of this and of his other
works have been preserved.

>   *Strabo :* (*a*) The country (*i.e.* Armenia) is so
> excellently suited to the rearing of horses, being not
> inferior indeed to Media, that the Nisæan steeds are
> raised there also of the same breed that the Persian
> kings were wont to use. And the satrap of Armenia
> used to send annually to Persia twice ten thousand
> colts for the Mithraic festivals.

(*b*) The Persians therefore do not erect statues
and altars, but sacrifice on a high place, regarding
the heaven as Zeus; and they honour also the sun,
whom they call Mithra, and the moon and Aphrodite
and fire and earth and the winds and water.

The extracts are from the *Geographika* of Strabo,
circa 20 B.C., books XI. 14, XV. 3. The author is supposed
to have in view here the passage from Herodotus cited
above (p. 24), and tacitly to correct the error which
makes of Mithra a female deity.

Pliny : (*a*) Mithrax is brought from Persia and
the hill-country of the Red Sea, a stone of varied
colours that reflects the light of the sun.

(*b*) The Assyrians prize Eumitren the jewel of Bel
their most honoured deity, of a light-green colour
and employed in divination.

The names of the precious stones described by Pliny
(*c*. 23–79 A.D.) seem to be derived from the name of the
god, and were probably therefore sacred to him and
worn or otherwise used in his ritual. The date of Pliny's
death, 79 A.D., is the year of the great eruption of
Vesuvius, in which he perished. The extracts are from
the last, the 37th book of the *Historia Naturalis*, Chap. X.

Quintus Curtius : The king himself with his
generals and Staff passed around the ranks of the
armed men, praying to the sun and Mithra and the
sacred eternal fire to inspire them with courage
worthy of their ancient fame and the monuments of
their ancestors.

Quintus Curtius Rufus wrote a History of Alexander
the Great in ten books, *c*. 40 to 50 A.D. The words

c

quoted are from the 4th Book, ch. 13.   The king is
Darius, reviewing his troops before the battle of Arbela,
331 B.C.

Plutarch : (a) The following is the opinion of the
great majority of learned men.   By some it is maintained that there are two gods, rivals as it were,
authors the one of good and the other of evil.   Others
confine the name of god to the good power, the other
they term demon, as was done by Zoroaster the
Magian, who is said to have lived to old age five
thousand years before the Trojan war.   He calls
the one Horomazes, the other Areimanius.   The
former he assserts is of all natural phenomena most
closely akin to the light, the latter to darkness, and
that Mithra holds an intermediate position.   To
Mithra therefore the Persians give the name of the
mediator.   Moreover he taught men to offer to
Horomazes worthy and unblemished sacrifices, but
to Areimanius imperfect and deformed.   For they
bruise a kind of grass called *molu* in a trough, and
invoke Hades and Darkness;   then mixing it with
the blood of a slaughtered wolf they carry it to a
sunless place and throw it away.   For they regard
some plants as the property of the good god, and
some of the evil demon;   and so also such animals
as dogs and birds and hedgehogs belong to the good
deity, and the water rat to the evil.   Of these last
therefore it is meritorious to kill as many as possible.

They have also many stories to relate concerning
the gods, for example that Horomazes was born of the
purest light, Areimanius of the darkness, and these are
hostile to one another. The former created six gods, the
first three deities respectively of good-will, truth, and
orderliness, the others of wisdom, wealth, and a good

conscience.[1] By the latter rivals as it were to these were
formed of equal number. Then Horomazes extended
himself to thrice his stature as far beyond the sun
as the sun is beyond the earth, and adorned the heaven
with stars, appointing one star, Sirius, as guardian
and watcher before all. He made also other twenty-
four gods and placed them in an egg, but Areimanius
produced creatures of equal number and these
crushed the egg . . . wherefore evil is mingled with
good. At the appointed time however Areimanius
must be utterly brought to nought and destroyed by
the pestilence and famine which he has himself
caused, and the earth will be cleared and made free
from obstruction, the habitation of a united community of men dwelling in happiness and speaking
one tongue. Theopompus further reports that
according to the magi for three thousand years in
succession each of the gods holds sway or is in sub-
jection, and that there will follow on these a further
period of three thousand years of war and strife, in
which they mutually destroy the works of one another.
Finally Hades will be overthrown, and men will be
blessed, and will neither need nourishment nor cast
a shadow.[2] And the deity who has accomplished
these things will then take rest and solace for a
period that is not long, especially for a god, and

[1] The last words are a paraphrase rather than a translation
of Plutarch's expression, τὸν τῶν ἐπὶ τοῖς καλοῖς ἡδέων δημιουργόν,
creator of the satisfaction derived from well-doing, or from noble
deeds. The meaning is doubtful. Plutarch was apparently
rendering a Persian title, the real significance of which had been
imperfectly conveyed to him; and his Greek reflects the obscurity
or ambiguity of the source on which he relied. The last of the
six Amshaspands, whose name or title would be expected here,
was *Ameretât*, deathlessness or immortality.

[2] *I. e.* they will be like the gods, of whom this is a charac-
teristic.

moderate for a sleeping man. To this effect then is
the legendary account given by the magi.

(b) If thou art not false to the interests of the
Persians, but remainest loyal to me thy lord, tell me
by thy regard for the great light of Mithra, and the
royal right hand. . . .

(c) Presenting a pomegranate of great size a certain
Omisus said to him : By Mithra you may trust this
man quickly to make an insignificant city great.

(d) They were accustomed to offer strange sacrifices on Olympus and to observe certain secret rites,
of which that of Mithra is maintained to the present
day by those by whom it was first established.

(e) Near it also (i.e. the Araxes) is a mountain
Diorphus, so called from the giant of that name, of
which this story is told : Mithra being desirous of a
son, and hating the female race, entered into a certain
rock ; and the stone becoming pregnant after the
appointed time bore a child named Diorphus. The
latter when he had grown to manhood challenged
Ares to a contest of valour, and was slain. The
purpose of the gods was then fulfilled in his trans-
formation into the mountain which bears his name.

The first passage is from the *De Iside et Osiride*, ch. 46.
It is doubtful on what sources or authorities Plutarch
relies for his description of the Persian rites and religion.
He names Theopompus, the Greek historian of the
4th century B.C., but does not appear to claim his
authority for the entire account. For the details and
legends he seems to be dependent in part at least upon
vague tradition or report. Attention is called by
Cumont to the mention of μῶλυ = haoma as of interest,
and possibly pointing to other than a Persian source, for

μῶλυ is said to be a Cappadocian word. Plutarch himself was born at Chæronea in Bœotia in or shortly before the year 50 A.D., and lived to the age of seventy or more years.

The other passages are taken respectively from the Lives of Alexander, Artaxerxes Mnemon, and Pompey, and from the *De Fluviis*, XXIII, 4.

Dion Chrysostom, *c.* 100 A.D., a philosophical writer under the emperors Nerva and Trajan, composed a series of discourses or essays (λόγοι) on various subjects, in one of which he reports concerning the doctrines and practices of the magi. It is uncertain, however, whether his narrative has any direct reference to the cult of Mithra. Cumont quotes it with a few others among " doubtful texts." Its interest justifies its insertion here.

Dion Chrysostom : In the secret mysteries the magi relate a further marvellous tradition concerning this god (Zeus) that he was the first and faultless charioteer of the unrivalled car. For they declare that the car of the sun is more recent, but on account of its prominent course in the sky is familiar to all. Whence is derived, it would seem, the common legend adopted by almost all the leading poets who have told of the risings and settings of the sun, the yoking of the steeds, and his ascent into the car. But of the mighty and perfect car of Zeus none of our writers hitherto has worthily sung, not even Homer or Hesiod, but the story is told by Zoroaster and the descendants of the magi who have learnt from him. Of him the Persians relate that moved by love of wisdom and righteousness he separated himself from men and lived apart on a certain

mountain, that fire subsequently fell from heaven
and the whole mountain was kindled into flame. The
king then with the most illustrious of the Persians
approached wishing to offer prayer to the god.
And Zoroaster came forth from the fire unharmed,
and gently bade them be of good courage and offer
certain sacrifices, since it was the divine sanctuary
to which the king had come. Afterwards only
those distinguished for love of the truth and who
were worthy to approach the god were permitted to
have access, and to these the Persians gave the name
of magi, as being adepts in the divine service;
differing therein from the Greeks who through
ignorance of the name call such men wizards.[1]
And among other sacred rites they maintain for
Zeus a pair of Nisæan steeds, these being the noblest
and strongest that Asia yields, but one steed only
for the sun. Moreover, they recount their legend
not like our poets of the Muses who with all the arts
of persuasion endeavour to carry conviction, but
quite simply. For without doubt the control and
government of the Supreme [2] are unique, actuated
always by the highest skill and strength, and that
without cessation through endless ages. The circuits
then of the sun and moon are, as I said, movements
of parts, and therefore readily discernible; most
men however do not understand the movement
and course of the whole, but the majestic order of
its succession removes it above their comprehension.
The further stories which they tell concerning the
steeds and their management I hesitate to relate;

---

[1] ἀνθρώπους γόητας.

[2] τοῦ σύμπαντος, the universal, all in all. There is supposed
to be a reference to the λόγος of the Stoics.

and indeed they fail to take into account that the
nature of the symbolism they employ betrays their
own character. For it may be that it would be
regarded as an act of folly for me to set forth a
barbarian tale by the side of the fair Greek lays.
I must however make the venture. The first of
the steeds is said to surpass infinitely in beauty and
size and swiftness, running as it does on the outside
round of the course, sacred to Zeus himself; and it
is winged. The colour also of its skin is bright, of
the purest sheen. And on it the sun and the moon
are emblematically represented; I understand the
meaning to be that these steeds have emblems
moon-shaped or other; and they are seen by us
indistinctly like sparks dancing in the bright blaze
of a fire, each with its own proper motion. And the
other stars receive their light through it and are
all under its influence; and some have the same
motion and are carried round with it, and others
follow different courses. And the latter have each
their own name among men, but the others are
grouped together, assigned to certain forms and
shapes. The most handsome and variegated steed
then is the favourite of Zeus himself, and on this
account is lauded by them, receiving as is right the
chief sacrifices and honours. The next to it in rank
bears the name of Hera, being tractable and gentle,
greatly inferior however in strength and swiftness.
Its colour is naturally black, but that which is
illuminated by the sun is always resplendent, while
that which is in shadow during its circuit reveals
the true character of the skin. The third is sacred
to Poseidon, and is slower in movement than the
second. His counterpart the poets say is found

among men, meaning I suppose that which bears
the name of Pegasus; a spring,[1] according to the
story, breaking forth in Corinth when the ground
was opened. The fourth is the strangest figure of
all, fixed and motionless, not furnished with wings,
named Hestia; but they do not hesitate to declare
that this also is yoked to the car, remaining however
in its place champing a bit of steel. And the others
are on each side closely attached to it, the two
nearest turning equally towards it, as though
assailing it and resenting its control; but the leader
on the outside circles constantly around it as though
around a fixed centre post. For the most part
therefore they live in peace and amity unhurt by
one another, but eventually after a long time and
many circuits the powerful breath of the leader
descends from above and kindles into flame the
proud spirit of the others, and most of all of the
last. His flaming mane [2] then is set on fire, in
which he took especial pride, and the whole universe.
This calamity which they record they say that the
Greeks attribute to Phaethon, for they refuse to
blame Zeus' driving of the car, and are unwilling to
attach fault to the circuits of the sun . . . and
again when in the course of further years the sacred
colt of the Nymphs and Poseidon rouses itself to
unaccustomed exertion, and incommoded with the
sweat that pours from it drenches its own yokefellow,

---

[1] πήγασος, the name being connected with or derived from
πήγη. Pegasus was said to be the son of Poseidon.
[2] χαίτη, i. e. the vegetation, grass and trees of the earth,
kindled by the breath of the supreme god. In the Mithraic
sculptures the lion-headed god is sometimes represented with
flame proceeding out of his mouth. There is supposed also to
be a reference to, or confusion with the Stoic conception of
periodical devastation of the world by fire.

it gives rise to a destruction the contrary of the preceding, a flood of water. This then is the one catastrophe of which the Greeks have record owing to their recent origin and the shortness of their memory, and they relate that Deucalion reigned over them at that time before the universal destruction. And in consequence of the ruin brought upon themselves men regard these rare occurrences as taking place neither in harmony with reason nor as a part of the general order, overlooking the fact that they occur in due course and in accordance with the will of the preserver and ruler of all. For it is just as when a charioteer chastises one of his steeds by checking it with the rein or touching it with the whip; the horse gives a start and is restless before settling down into its accustomed order. This earlier control then of the team they say is firm and the universe suffers no harm; but later a change takes place in the movement of the four, and their natures are mutually altered and interchanged, until they are all subdued by the higher power and a uniform character is imposed on all. Nevertheless they do not hesitate to compare this movement to the conduct and driving of a car, for lack of a more impressive simile. As though a clever artificer should fashion horses out of wax, and should then smooth off the roughnesses of each, adding now to one and now to another, finally reducing all to one pattern, and forming his whole material into one shape. This however is not the case of a Creator fashioning and transforming from the outside the material substance of things without life, but the experience is that of the very substances themselves, as though they were contending for victory in a real

and well-contested strife; and the crown of victory
is awarded of right to the first and foremost in
swiftness and strength and in every kind of virtue,
to whom at the beginning of our discourse we gave
the name of " chosen of Zeus." For this one being
the strongest and naturally fiery quickly consumed
the others as though they had been really wax in
a period not actually long, though to our limited
reasoning it appears infinite; and absorbing into
himself the entire substance of all is seen to be far
greater and more glorious than before, having won
the victory in the most formidable contest by no
mortal or immortal aid, but by his own valour.
Raised then proudly aloft and exulting in his victory,
he takes possession of the widest possible domain,
and yet such is his might and power that he craves
further room for expansion. Having reached this
conclusion they shrink [1] from describing the nature
of the living creature as the same; for that it is now
no other than the soul of the charioteer and lord, or
rather it has the same purpose and mind.

There is some doubt whether the words of Chrysostom
imply a recognition of Magian practices or of later
Mithraism. The basis of his exposition and cosmological
doctrine is Stoic. But there are features that seem to
be directly attributable to the Magi and the mystical
teaching of the East, for example the repeated destruction of the universe and the rivalry and strife of the
four elements. See Cumont's notes on the passage.

Statius : Whether it please thee to bear the name
of ruddy Titan after the manner of the Achæmenian

[1] Read probably οὐ δυσωποῦνται, they do not shrink from.

race, or Osiris lord of the crops, or Mithra as beneath
the rocks of the Persian cave he presses back the
horns that resist his control.

Scholiast : (*a*) He declares that different nations
give to Apollo different names. The Achæmenians
call him Titan, the Egyptians Osiris, the Persians
Mithra and worship him in a cave. The expression
" resist his control " has reference to the figure of
Mithra holding back the horns of a recalcitrant
bull, whereby is indicated the sun's illumination of
the moon, when the latter receives its rays.

(*b*) The Egyptians regard Osiris as the sun, by
whom they think success may be assured to the
crops. . . . These rites were first observed by the
Persians, from whom the Phrygians received them,
and from the Phrygians the Romans. The Persians
give to the sun the native name of Mithra, as
Hostanes relates.

(*c*) The Persians are known as Achæmenians
from Achæmenes, son of Perseus and Andromeda,
who ruled there. They call the sun Apollo, and are
said to have initiated the rites in his honour.

(*d*) The Persians are said to have been the first to
worship the sun in caverns. For he is represented
in a cavern in Persian dress with a turban, grasping
the horns of a bull with both hands. The figure is
interpreted of the moon; for reluctant to follow his
brother he meets him full and his light is obscured.
In these verses the mysteries of the rites of the sun
are set forth. For in proof that the moon is
inferior and of less power the sun is seated on the
bull and grasps its horns. By which words Statius
intended the two-horned moon to be understood,
not the animal on which he rides.

(e) The meaning is as follows: The Persians worship the Sun in caverns, and this sun is in their own language known as Mithra, who as suffering eclipse is worshipped within a cave. The sun himself moreover is represented with the face of a lion with turban and in Persian dress, with both hands grasping the horns of an ox. And this figure is interpreted of the moon, which reluctant to follow its brother meets him full and obscures his light. He has revealed further a part of the mysteries. The Sun therefore presses down the bull as though to show [1] that the moon is inferior. He has laid especial stress moreover on the horns, in order that attention may be more clearly called to the moon, and not to the animal on which she is represented as riding. Since however this is not the place to discuss the mysteries of those gods on the lines of an abstract philosophy, I will add a few words with regard to the symbols employed. The sun is supreme, and because he treads down and controls the chief constellation, that is to say the lion, he is himself represented with this face; or the reason may be that he surpasses the rest of the gods in power and energy, as the lion other wild beasts, or because of its impetuosity. The moon however being nearer to the bull controls and leads it, and is represented as a cow. But these gods of divine and royal estate as they appear in the world are without mortal form either of man or beast, having neither beginning nor end nor an intermediate part as other and lesser deities, as he himself declares above: " next comes the crowd of the wandering demigods." For that is necessitated by the attribute of eternity.

[1] Cumont would adopt the correction *ducens* for *docens*, possibly rightly.

(*f*) He gives to the rocks of a Persian cavern the name of temple of Perseus in virtue of the representation there of Phœbus as drawing to himself the moon that is reluctant to follow. After the full moon the latter goes in advance of the sun, and in so doing gradually loses her own light, until she ceases entirely to shine. Approaching the sun however at length she renews her light, and then follows the sun. Moreover at the full, being now nearest to the sun, she is said to be grasped by him.

P. Papinius Statius, who lived in the second half of the first century, spent the greater part of his life in Rome, but returned to his native city of Naples towards the end of the century, and seems to have died there *c.* 96 A.D. His principal work is an epic poem on the expedition of the Seven against Thebes, modelled on Virgil. Besides the Thebais, Statius composed also an Achilleis of which a part only has been preserved, and a collection of shorter poems, epigrammatic or panegyric, under the title of *Silvæ*. The lines quoted are from Theb. I. 717 ff. The commentary is attributed to Lactantius Placidus, a grammarian, who seems to have lived in the fifth century; but it is almost certainly a compilation.

Justin Martyr : (*a*) Accordingly in the mysteries of Mithra also we have heard that evil spirits practise mimicry. For at the initiatory rites bread and a cup of water are set out accompanied by certain formulæ, as you know or may ascertain.

(*b*) And when in the tradition of the Mithraic mysteries they relate that Mithra was born of a rock, and name the place where his followers receive initiation a cave, do I not know that they are per-

verting the saying of Daniel that " a stone was hewn
without hands from a great mountain," [1] and like-
wise the words of Isaiah,[2] all whose sayings also
they endeavour to pervert ?   Noteworthy sayings too
besides these they have artfully contrived to use.

(c) According to the tradition of the Mithraic
mysteries initiation takes place among them in a
so-called cave, . . . a device of the evil one.

The quotations from Justin are taken from *Apol.*
I, 66, and *Dial. c. Tryph.* chs. 70 and 78.   The Apology
is addressed to the Emperor Antoninus Pius, and was
written *c.* 150 A.D., probably a year or two earlier;
Apol. II followed at no long interval.   There is nothing
to fix the date of the Dialogue with Trypho.   It is
generally supposed to be later than the Apologies.   The
year of Justin's birth also at Neapolis, or Nablus, near
the ancient Sychem, is uncertain.   According to Epiphanius he was thirty years of age at the time of his
martyrdom, but the tradition is uncorroborated, and no
direct evidence exists.   Justin argues that the Mithraic
rites are a parody of the Christian.

Lucian : (a) And Attis too, by heaven, and
Korybas and Sabazius with what a flood have these
deluged us, and your Mithra with his Assyrian cloak
and crown, maintaining even their foreign tongue,
so that when they give a toast no one can understand
what they say.

(b) There is Bendis herself and Anubis yonder and
by his side Attis and Mithra and Men, all resplendent
in gold, weighty and costly you may be sure.

(c) Once as with these thoughts I was lying awake

---

[1] Dan. ii. 34.   [2] Is. xxxiii. 16.

I determined to go to Babylon and there make inquiry of one of the magi, the disciples and successors of Zoroaster. I had heard that by incantations and magic rites they open the gates of Hades, and lead thither in safety whom they will, and restore him again to the upper world . . . so I arose at once, and without delay set out for Babylon. On arrival I betook myself to a certain Chaldæan, a man skilled in the art of the diviner, grey-haired and wearing an imposing beard, whose name was Mithrobarzanes. With much trouble and importunity I won his consent, for whatever fee he liked to name, to be my guide on the way. He took me under his charge, and first for twenty-nine days from the new moon he conducted me at dawn to the Euphrates and bathed me, reciting some long invocation to the rising sun, which I did not fully understand; for like the second-rate heralds at the games he spoke in obscure and involved fashion. It was clear however that he was invoking certain deities. Then after the invocation he spat thrice in front of me and conducted me back without looking in the face of any whom we met. For food we had acorns, and our drink was milk and honey-mead and the waters of the Choaspes, and we made our couch upon the grass in the open air. These preliminaries concluded he took me about midnight to the Tigris, cleansed and rubbed me down and purified me with resinous twigs and hyssop and many other things, reiterating at the same time the previous invocation. Then he threw spells over me and circumambulated me for my defence against the ghosts and led me back to the house, as I was, on foot; and the rest of the journey we made by boat.

He himself put on some sort of a Magian robe, not unlike that of the Medes. And he further equipped me with the cap and lion's skin and put into my hands the lyre, and bade me if I were asked my name not to answer Menippus, but to say Herakles or Odysseus or Orpheus. . . . Arrived at a certain place, gloomy and desolate and overgrown with jungle, we disembarked, Mithrobarzanes leading the way, and dug a pit, and sacrificed the sheep, pouring out the blood over it. Then the Magian with lighted torch in his hand, no longer in subdued tones but exerting his voice to the utmost, invoked the whole host of demons with the Avengers and Furies, " and Hecate the queen of night and noble Persephone," joining with them some foreign names of inordinate length.

Lucian of Samosata, c. 120–200 A.D., travelled much not only in Greece but in the West, in France and Italy, and later in Egypt. His literary work, however, was done for the most part in Athens where he settled in middle life. His dialogues are satires, directed against the popular religions and their gods, and to unmask the ignorance which lays claim to the possession of knowledge. In language Lucian attempted to reproduce the Attic Greek of literature in an age when this had long been superseded by the κοινή. The passages are from the Council of the Gods (Θεῶν διάλογοι, ch. IX), the Tragic Zeus (Ζεὺς τραγῳδός, ch. VIII), and the Menippus (Μένιππος, ch. VI). In the last Menippus has been disappointed in his quest of wisdom from the professing philosophers, and has recourse to foreign magic.

Tertullian : (a) For nations destitute of all understanding of spiritual powers attribute the same efficacy to their idols; but they cheat themselves with springs that yield no living water. For in certain rites also of an Isis or Mithra initiation is by means of baptismal water.

(b) Be ashamed as Christ's fellow-soldiers to be open to reproach not only from Christ himself but from any soldier of Mithra. For to him when he is initiated in a cavern, a veritable home of darkness, a crown is offered on a naked sword, as if in parody of martyrdom; this then is placed on his head, and he is enjoined with his own hand to lift it from his head and voluntarily to transfer it to his shoulder, declaring that Mithra is his crown. Thereafter he is never crowned. And this is regarded as evidence of his steadfastness, if ever he is tempted to break his oath, and forthwith he is regarded as a soldier of Mithra, should he have rejected the crown and claimed the god himself as his crown. We may recognise the craft of the devil, who counterfeits divine things to turn us from our faith and bring us into condemnation.

(c) The lions of Mithra are represented as types of an eager and impetuous nature.

(d) The devil (is the inspirer of the heretics) whose work it is to pervert the truth, who with idolatrous mysteries endeavours to imitate the realities of the divine sacraments. Some he himself sprinkles as though in token of faith and loyalty; he promises forgiveness of sins through baptism; and if my memory does not fail me marks his own soldiers with the sign of Mithra on their foreheads, commemorates an offering of bread, introduces a mock resurrection, and with the sword opens the way to

D

the crown.   Moreover has he not forbidden a second
marriage to the supreme priest?   He maintains also
his virgins and his celibates.

(e) Those who aspire to initiation first I believe
approach the father of the ceremonies to learn from
him the preparations that are to be made.

Tertullian was born of heathen parents at Carthage
about the year 150 A.D. and lived to the age of seventy
or more years.   The exact dates of his birth and death
are unknown.   A scholar and a saint, he found in
Christianity the satisfaction and assurance which the
philosophy and practice of his day failed to give, and
his writings are the forceful *apologia* for his own life
and thought.   The first quotation is from the *De
Baptismo*, ch. V; the second from the *De Coronâ*,
ch. XV; the remainder are respectively from *Adv.
Marcionem*, I. 13, *De Præscriptione Hæreticorum*, 40,
and *Apol*. VIII.   In the last the reference to the father
of the ceremonies (*pater sacrorum*) is usually understood
of the votaries of Mithra.

> *Dion Cassius:* I, my lord, am son of Arsaces,
> and brother of the kings Vologeses and Pacoras, and
> thy servant. And I am come to thee as my god, to
> worship thee as I worship Mithra, and I will be as
> thou shalt determine. For thou art my Destiny
> and my Fate.

The speaker is the Armenian king, Tiridates, address-
ing Nero.   The Roman History (Ῥωμαϊκὴ Ἱστορία) of
Dion Cassius, *c*. 200 A.D., an elaborate work in eighty
or more books, preserved only in part, narrated the
history of Rome from the earliest period to the year

229 A.D. The passage quoted is from the sixty-third book, ch. 10.

Origen : (a) Celsus urges that argument and reason compel us to accept certain dogmas, on the ground that those who refuse their assent are without doubt the victims of error. And he likens those who believe without reason to tramps and fortune-tellers, to followers of Mithra or Sabazius, or to any chance guide, unsubstantial forms of Hecate or other demon or demons.

(b) Celsus following Plato affirms that souls proceed to and from the earth by way of the planets . . . and further being desirous of exhibiting his learning in controversy with us he expounds certain Persian mysteries also, and among them the following : " These doctrines are contained in the traditions of the Persians and in the cult of Mithra which they practise. For the latter gives a kind of representation of the two heavenly spheres, the one fixed and the other assigned to the planets, and of the journey of the soul through these. There is an ascending road with seven gates, and an eighth at the summit. The first gate is of lead, the second of tin, the third of bronze, the fourth of iron, the fifth of mixed metal, the sixth of silver, and the seventh of gold. The first is dedicated to Kronus, the lead symbolizing the planet's slow motion. The second to Aphrodite, the resemblance consisting in the bright and malleable nature of the tin. The third, firm and resistant, to Zeus. The fourth to Hermes, in that like the iron Hermes is the tireless and efficient worker and producer of wealth. The fifth to Ares, because of the variable and irregular nature of the alloy. The sixth,

of silver, to the Moon; and the seventh, of gold, to
the Sun, from a comparison of their colours." Later
Celsus investigates the reason for this definite assign-
ment of the stars in whose names the remainder of
the physical universe finds symbolical expression,
and he expounds further the doctrines of harmony
in which the Persian theology is set forth. In
addition to these he is so ambitious as to publish a
second treatise dealing with the principles of music.
In my judgement however, for Celsus to propound
his theory in these is absurd; it is like his procedure
in the matter of his denunciation of Christians and
Jews where he makes irrelevant quotations from
Plato, and is so far from being satisfied with these
that he drags in the Persian mysteries as he calls
them of Mithra also with all their details. For
whether these things are true or false in the belief of
those who preside over the Mithraic rites of the
Persians, why did he choose them for exposition
and interpretation rather than any other mysteries?
for Greeks have no preference for mysteries of
Mithra rather than those of Eleusis or the traditional
rites of Hecate which they celebrate in Aegina. And
why if he felt it incumbent upon him to set forth
foreign mysteries did he not rather prefer the
Egyptian, in which many take an interest, or the
Cappadocian worship of Artemis in Comana, or the
Thracian, or even those of the Romans themselves
in which the most high-born senators take part?
but if he regarded it as unsuitable to his purpose to
adopt any one of these on the ground that they
furnished no support to his denunciation of Jews or
Christians, how is it that he did not draw the same
conclusion with regard to his exposition of the
Mithraic rites?

The quotations are from the *Refutation of Celsus*, I. 9 and VI. 21. Origen was born at Alexandria *c.* 185 A.D., and died in his seventieth year at Tyre, where also according to the Christian tradition he was buried. The *Contra Celsum* in eight books was one of his latest works, written not long before his death.

Clement : Adonis also they take to represent the ripe fruits, Aphrodite birth and marriage, Demeter the soil, Kore the seeds, and some regard Dionysus as the vine. All explanations of this nature alike imply in my judgement a kind of metaphor. Apollo is to be regarded as the sun in his course, the offspring of Zeus, named also Mithra, as he completes the cycle of the year.

The *Homilies*, erroneously attributed to Clement of Rome, are usually ascribed to the end of the second century, and were originally composed probably in Syria. The quotation is from the 6th book, ch. 9-10.

Porphyry : (*a*) Our ancestors appear to have adorned and consecrated grottos and caves . . . so the Persians also initiate the novice into the mysteries by an allegorical descent of the souls to the lower world and a return, and they use the name cave. In the first instance, according to the report of Eubulus, Zoroaster consecrated a natural cave in the adjacent mountains of Persis, carpeted with grass and with fresh springs, to the honour of Mithra creator and father of all, in imitation of the world-cave which Mithra fashioned, and of the natural elements and regions which bore within at regular intervals symbolic representations. And after Zoroaster the custom was observed amongst others also

of celebrating their rites in grottos and caves either
natural or artificial.

(*b*) The votaries use honey for many and diverse
symbolic purposes, because of its variety of pro-
perties, since it possesses both purgative and pre-
serving virtue. For by honey many things are
preserved from corruption and wounds of long
standing are cleansed. It is also sweet to the taste
and is gathered from flowers by bees which are
regarded as born of cattle. When therefore into
the hands of those initiated into the lion grade
honey is poured for washing instead of water, they
are charged to keep their hands clean from all wrong
and injury and defilement; the offering of actual
water to the initiate is avoided as being hostile
to the fire with its purifying qualities. The tongue
also is purified from all sin by honey. And when
honey is offered to the Persian [1] as the guardian of
the fruits, its preservative virtue is symbolically
expressed.

(*c*) The bowls symbolize the springs, as in the
ritual of Mithra the bowl is set for the spring. . . .
Our ancestors used to call the priestesses of Demeter,
as being an earth goddess, mystic bees, and the
maiden herself honied; to the moon also as presiding
over birth they gave the name of bee, especially
since the moon is a bull and the moon culminates in
the Bull, and bees are bull-begotten. And souls
when they come to birth are bull-begotten, and the
god who secretly promotes [2] birth is a stealer of
bulls.

[1] *I.e.* the fifth grade of initiation, see p. 61.
[2] The text is λεληθότως ἀκούων which can hardly be right. Of
the many suggestions that have been made perhaps βοηθῶν is the
best: gives aid in birth.

(d) Our earliest ancestors therefore, before temples were invented, used to consecrate to the gods recesses and caves in Crete to the Zeus of the Curetes, in Arcadia to Selene and the Lycæan Pan, and in Naxos to Dionysus. And wherever Mithra is known, the sanctuary where he is worshipped is a cave.

(e) He (i.e. Homer) has not described the entrances therefore by east or west or by the equinoxes, i.e. by the ram and the scales, but by north and south (gates opening to the south being most exposed to wet, those to the north to cold), because the cave is sacred to souls and the water-nymphs, and the regions of birth and death appertain to souls. Mithra's own seat however is determined by the equinoxes. He bears therefore the sword of the ram, the Aries of the zodiac, and rides on Aphrodite's bull, since the bull is generator and he (Mithra) is lord of creation. Moreover according to the equinoctial cycle he is represented with the north on his right and the south on his left, his southern hemisphere being so assigned because of its warmth, his northern because of the cold of the wind. And to souls that come to the birth and depart from life it was natural to assign winds, because they also bring with them breath, as some have supposed, and are of similar nature. But the north is appropriate to those that come to the birth.

(f) Pallas declares that under the emperor Hadrian human sacrifices were almost entirely abolished; and he is the best exponent of the mysteries of Mithra.[1]

---

[1] Cp. Euseb., *Prep. Evang.* IV. 16. 7. It is not implied of course that human sacrifice was countenanced by the Mithraic ritual.

(g) Among the Persians those who are learned in the doctrines of the gods and minister in their service bear the name of magi. For this is the meaning of magian in their native tongue. And this class has been regarded among the Persians as so great and honourable that Darius Hystaspes had inscribed upon his tomb in addition to his other titles that he had been a teacher of Magian lore. The magi were divided into three grades, according to the assertion of Eubulus who wrote the history of Mithraism in many books. Of these the highest and most learned neither kill nor eat any living thing, but practise the long-established abstinence from animal food. The second use such food, but do not kill any tame beasts. And following their example not even the third permit themselves the use of all. For in all the highest grades the doctrine of metempsychosis is held, which also is apparently signified in the mysteries of Mithra; for these through the living creatures reveal to us symbolically our community of nature with them. So the mystics who take part in the actual rites are called lions, the women hyænas, the servants crows, and of the fathers . . . for these bear the names of eagles and hawks. He who is invested with the character of the lion adopts various forms of living creatures, the reason of which is said by Pallas in his work on Mithra to be the belief in their common life-history, which extends over the course of the zodiacal cycle; and a true and precise conception of human souls is set forth in symbol, for these they say pass through various bodies.

Porphyry was a philosopher of the Neo-Platonic school

of Tyrian origin born about the year 232 A.D. He
spent most of his life in Rome and Sicily, and died
according to the tradition at the age of seventy or
more years in the former city. The *De Abstinentia*,
from which the last two extracts are taken (II. 56,
IV. 16), is the most important of his philosophical works
that has been preserved. The other passages are quoted
from the *De Antro Nympharum*, a brief treatise more or
less serious on mythological topics : (*a*) chs. 5–6;
(*b*) ch. 15; (*c*) ch. 18; (*d*) ch. 20; (*e*) ch. 24. Porphyry
moreover seems to be the only writer who makes reference to women initiates into the service and rites of
Mithra, and his allusion is perhaps due to a misunder-
standing. In the text (*g*) λέαιναs, lionesses, should
probably be read for ὕαιναs. The participation of women
in the ritual was not unknown in the Eastern cults, but
the predominant military influence in Mithraism seems
to render it unlikely in this instance.

Commodian : Whether the invincible, born from
a rock, is to be regarded as divine—I now pronounce
no judgement; it is for you to decide which of
these has the priority. If the rock preceded the
god, who then was the rock's creator? Moreover
you portray him as a thief. Yet surely were he
divine he would not be guilty of theft. The truth
is he was of earthly birth and shared the nature of
the creature, and was always driving off another's
bullocks in his caves, like Cacus of the story the
fabled son of Vulcan.

Commodian was a Christian writer of the third
century, the author of two works in irregular hexameters : (1) *Carmen apologeticum*, against Jewish and

heathen beliefs, composed probably in the year 249 A.D.;
(2) *Instructiones*, consisting of eighty short acrostic
poems in two books, written perhaps a year or two
later. The first book is similar in content and aim to
the Carmen, the second is doctrinal and hortative. The
poem quoted is the thirteenth of the first book, the
initial letters of the Latin lines forming the word
Invictus. The reference to the theft is to the traditional
story of Mithra's harrying and carrying off the oxen of
the Sun; see Introd., p. 13 f.

> *Arnobius :* It is not right to assert or maintain a
> likeness where the main features do not show similar
> lines. . . . The sun is clearly seen by all men to be
> smooth and rounded, but you ascribe to him human
> face and features. The moon is always in motion,
> and assumes thrice ten forms in her changing monthly
> circuit. According to your representation she is a
> woman, with a countenance that does not alter,
> though her daily variation carries her through a
> thousand forms. We all know that the winds are
> pulsations of the atmosphere, set in motion and
> stirred by mundane forces. You give them the faces
> of men with cheeks distended with the violent blasts
> of their trumpets. Among your gods we see the
> grim face of a lion smeared with vine and bearing a
> name reminiscent of the crops.[1]

Arnobius does not name Mithra, but has been supposed to refer here to the lion-headed form of the
Mithraic god. The reference is however doubtful. No
similar description is found elsewhere and the " name
reminiscent of the crops " is otherwise applied to Saturn;

[1] Nomine frugiferio. Cumont however would adopt the
suggestion " frugiferi," *i.e.* Saturn.

compare the φύλαξ καρπῶν of Porphyry (*sup.* p. 48).
The lion-headed god seems however to have been
identified with Saturn.

Arnobius, a Christian apologist and rhetorician, composed seven books, *Adversus Nationes*, in or about the
year 295 A.D. The date of his birth is uncertain, but
he seems to have lived thirty years or more after the
publication of his apology. The words quoted are from
bk. VII. 10.

Pseudo-Callisthenes : (*a*) I, Darius, king of kings and
of the race of the gods, consort of Mithra on his
throne and co-partner with the sun, in my own
right divine do give these injunctions and commands
to thee my servant Alexander.

(*b*) Alexander the king, the son of king Philip and
Olympias his mother, to the great king of the
Persians, king of kings and consort of the sun-god,
off-spring of the gods and co-partner with the sun,
greeting. It is unworthy that Darius, so great a
king of the Persians, exalted with so great power,
consort of the gods and co-partner with the sun,
should be reduced to mean servitude to a mere man
Alexander.

(*c*) Alexander then seeing the great pomp of
Darius was moved almost to worship him as Mithra
the divine, as though clothed in barbaric splendour
he had come down from heaven,—such was his
splendid array. Darius was seated upon a lofty
throne, with a crown of most precious stones, wearing a robe of Babylonian silk inwoven with golden
thread.

(Syriac) And when Darius saw Alexander he did
obeisance and worshipped Alexander, for he believed

that he was Mihr the god, and that he had come
down to bring aid to the Persians. For his raiment
was like that of the gods, and the crown which
rested upon his head shone with rays of light and
the robe which he wore was woven with fine gold.

(*d*) The Persians contended with the Macedonians,
wishing to carry off Alexander and to proclaim him
as Mithra. But the Macedonians resisted, wishing
to carry him back to Macedonia.

The date of the work from which the above extracts
are taken is uncertain. Callisthenes was a Greek
philosopher, the friend and adviser of Alexander the
Great, who was put to death *c.* 330 B.C. He was the
author of a history of Greece and other works, none of
which have been preserved. The legendary story to
which his name has been attached was put together,
probably in Egypt, in or about the close of the third
century of the Christian era. It seems to have circu-
lated mainly in the nearer east. Translations exist
more or less complete in Syriac, Armenian, Ethiopic,
and others, besides a Latin rendering by Julius Valerius
in the early part of the fourth century. The parallel
passages of the Latin and Syriac are cited by Cumont,
but except in (*c*) present no variations of interest. In
this passage the parts of Darius and Alexander have
been reversed. The references are I. 36, 39, II. 14,
III. 34.

Passages are quoted also by Cumont from magical
papyri of approximately the above date, which contain
the name Mithra and possible references to Mithraic
figures or ceremonies. They serve to show at least
that the name was sufficiently well-known and the god

credited with sufficient influence to make it worth while
to invoke him in incantations and prayer. The first is
from a magical papyrus text in the national library at
Paris, which is ascribed to the fourth century :

(a) Shew me favour, kindly Forethought (i.e.
Athene) and Fortune, as I write these ancient
mysteries that we have received, and for my only
son I beg [1] the gift of immortality, ye ministers of
this our great potency. You therefore, O daughter,
shouldest take the juices of herbs and of species
which are in thy care in the rite of my holy office.
For in this [2] the great sun-god Mithra bade me by
his archangel take part, that I . . . may rise to
heaven and have insight into all things. And of
my discourse this is the invocation. . . .

O king, greatest of the gods, thou sun, the lord of
heaven and earth, god of gods, thy breath is potent,
thy power is potent, if it seem good to thee, forward
me on my way to the supreme deity who begat
thee and formed thee, for I am the man N.

Also from a papyrus in the British Museum probably
of approximately the same date :

(b) I invoke thee, O Zeus the Sun-god Mithra
Sarapis, invincible, giver of mead, Melikertes, lord
of the mead, abraalbabachaebechi. . . .

It will be seen that there is no definite or certain
reference to Mithraism. The incantations are of the
usual form. It is only the mention of Mithra that gives
to them an immediate interest.

---

[1] Cumont prints ἀξίῳ. Read probably ἀξιῶ.
[2] ἥν, the antecedent appears to be τέλει although the gender
is in disagreement. If the reading is right the scribe of the
papyrus has made a mistake.

Hegemonius : What further then shall I say? You foreign priest and partner of Mithra you will worship Mithra alone as the sun, whose light penetrates and illuminates, as you imagine, the secret shrines. This worship it is that you travesty, and like a clever actor rehearse the mysteries.

The passage is from the Latin translation of a Greek polemical work directed against Manes and his false teaching in the earlier part of the fourth century. Of the writer himself nothing appears to be known. Read probably " coles . . .? " will you worship, as an indignant question.

Firmicus Maternus : (*a*) The Persians and all the magi who inhabit the borderlands of Persia reverence the fire, and give to it the primary place among all the elements. These then regard the fire as possessed of a double energy, assigning its character, to each sex, and expounding the essential substance of the fire under the figure of man and woman. The woman they represent with three faces and girded with huge snakes . . . while in their worship of the hero who drove off the bulls they transfer his rites to the cult of the fire, as his poet has recorded for us when he wrote :

Mystic priest of the captured bulls, skilful son of a noble sire.

To him they give the name of Mithra, and celebrate his rites in secret caves, that shrouded in the dim obscurity of the darkness they may shun the touch of the pure and glorious light. Truly an ill-omened exaltation of a deity ! a hateful recognition of a barbarian rule ! to deify one whose criminal acts you confess. When you affirm therefore that in the temples the magian rites are duly performed after the Persian ceremonial, why do you confine your approval to these Persian rites alone? If you think it not derogatory to the Roman name to adopt Persian cults and Persian laws. . . .

(b) The pass-word of a second mystery cult of foreign origin is the " god from the rock." Why do you shame your profession by transferring this sacred and revered name to heathen rites? Different indeed is the Stone which God in confirmation of his pledged word promised to send to Jerusalem. Under the figure of the sacred stone the Christ is represented to us. Why this deceitful and dishonourable transference of a revered name to unclean superstitions? . . . As for the stone of their idolatrous worship of which they use the title " God from the rock " what prophetic utterance has told thereof? To whom has that stone brought healing or mercy?

The Christian writer Firmicus Maternus about the middle of the fourth century addressed a tract to the Emperors Constantius and Constans, urging the destruction of paganism. *De Errore Profanarum Religionum*, chs. IV, XX.

Gregory Nazianzen : (a) The mutilations of the Phrygians distraught with the sound of the flute, and the tortures in the temple of Mithra, and the mystic cauteries, and the sacrifice of strangers among the Taurians.

(b) Neither the divination of the Magi, nor inspection of the victims, nor the astronomy and horoscopy of the Chaldæans . . . nor Thracian orgies . . . nor the mystic rites of Orpheus . . . nor the painful endurance required of the initiates of Mithra, nor the mutilations of Osiris . . . nor the misfortunes of Isis, etc.

(c) The mountain-haunting Bacchants in the train of Semele's son, and the ill-omened apparitions of nightly Hecate, and the shameful deeds and un-rivalled orgies of the Mithræan shrine.

Gregory of Nazianzus in Cappadocia studied at Athens, and was a versatile writer in the middle and latter part of the fourth century. The date of his birth is un-certain; it was certainly early in the century. A life of stress and anxiety ended in six years of retire-ment at Arianzus, where probably he died A.D. 389 or 390. In addition to his theological works he was the author of numerous poems on historical, ethical and doctrinal subjects. The first two passages given above are from the *Orationes* IV. *Adv. Julianum*, ch. LXX., and XXXIX. *In sancta Lumina*, ch. V.; the third is from a hexameter poem *Ad Nemesium*, VII. 265 ff. A few words quoted also by Cumont from a later chapter of the *Adv. Jul.* have certainly no reference to Mithraism, and the mention of Mithra in the text is probably a copyist's error.

Julian : (a) Were I to tell you next of the reve-rence paid to Mithra and the quadrennial games in honour of the sun I should be expounding a ritual of quite recent date. It would be better perhaps to set forth a cult of more ancient times.

(b) But to thee, Hermes declares to us, have I granted the knowledge of Mithra the father. Do thou therefore observe his commands, providing for thyself in this life a sure cable and anchorage, and with a joyous confidence assuring for thyself when thou departest hence the gracious guidance of the god.

(c) Were I also to make reference to the secret initiatory rite which the Chaldæan priest celebrates for the seven-rayed god, by whose aid he conducts the souls upwards, I should be telling of mysteries, mysteries at least to the vulgar, but within the knowledge of the fortunate hierophants. On these matters therefore for the present I will be silent.

(d) Immediately after the last month of Kronos and before the new moon we observe the renowned festival in honour of the Sun, celebrating the feast to the invincible Sun, after which none of the gloomy rites which the last month involves, necessary as they are, may be completed; but in the order of the cycle the festal days of the sun succeed immediately upon the last days of Kronos. May mine be the good fortune often to celebrate and to confirm these by the favour of the royal gods, and above others of the Sun himself the king of the universe.

The first and third passages are from the *Orationes* of the Emperor IV. 155 *b* and V. 172 *d*. The words of the second quotation are supposed to be addressed to the Emperor by Hermes at the close of a banquet on Olympus, *Cæsares aut Convivium* 336 *c*, in which Julian satirises his predecessors; the date of composition is 361–2 A.D. The festival to which reference is made in the last extract (*d*) is the annual feast in honour of the Sun at the end of the year. The relation, if any, of these yearly observances to the Mithraic ritual is uncertain. It is derived from *Orationes* IV., Εἰς τὸν Βασιλέα Ἥλιον, 156 *c*. Flavius Claudius Julianus was born at Constantinople in the year 331 A.D., reigned

E

for two years as Emperor, 361–363, and was killed in
battle against the Persians in the latter year not far from
Ctesiphon. In printing these brief extracts from his
works Cumont notes that it would have been easy to add
largely to them by including references to solar worship;
but these also are doubtfully connected with the special
cult of Mithra.

Himerius : (*a*) At the summons of the Emperor
Julian he went to the Emperor's camp for the purpose
of giving exhibitions of rhetoric in Constantinople.
Prior to the exhibition he was initiated into the
Mithraic mysteries, and delivered his oration before
the city and the Emperor who had established the
rite.

(*b*) With heart enlightened by Mithra the sun, and
by divine grace admitted now to friendship with the
king the friend of the gods, tell me what discourse
in the stead of a lamp we should kindle for the king
and the city.   For the law of Athens bids the mystics
carry a light and sheaves of corn to Eleusis, in token
of a blameless life.   But let our mystics present as
their thank-offering an oration, if indeed I am right
that Apollo is the Sun and that discourses are the
sons of Apollo.

(*c*) He (*i.e.* Julian) by his virtue dispelled the
darkness which forbade the uplifting of the hands
to the Sun, and as though from the cheerless life of
an underworld he gained a vision of the heavens,
when he raised shrines to the gods and established
divine rites that were strange to the city, and consecrated therein the mysteries of the heavenly
deities. And far and wide he bestowed no trifling
grants of healing, as the sick in body are revived by

human skill, but unlimited gifts of health. For with a nature akin to the sun he could not fail to shine and illuminate the way to a better life.

Himerius was born at Prusa in Bithynia, and practised rhetoric in Athens and Constantinople under the Emperors Constantius and Julian, in his old age losing his eyesight. In addition to *Orationes*, from which (*a*) is taken (VII. 60, A.D. 362), he composed a *Panegyric* on Julian and Constantinople, of which (*b*) is the opening words; (*c*) is from ch. IX. 62.

Jerome: (*a*) When a few years ago your relative Græcus, whose name bespeaks his noble birth, held the office of prefect of the city, did he not utterly destroy the cave of Mithra with all the monstrous crew that give names to the initiates in their grades, the crow, the gryphon, the soldier, the lion, the Persian, Heliodromus,[1] and father? These his works were pledges as it were sent forward, whereby he gained Christian baptism.

(*b*) According to the popular legend Mithra and Erichthonius were born in a rock or in the ground by the unaided passion of lust.

(*c*) Eubulus the author of a history of Mithra in many volumes states that there are three classes of magi among the Persians, the first of which, men pre-eminent in learning and eloquence, confine their food to pulse and vegetables alone.

(*d*) Basilides gives to the omnipotent god the uncouth name of Abraxas, and asserts that according

---

[1] For the name Cumont quotes an inscription from Otourah in Phrygia given in Ramsay, *Cities and Bishoprics of Phrygia*, vol. I., pt. ii, p. 566. The name is unknown elsewhere in connection with the Mithraic mysteries.

to the Greek letters and the number of the cycle of
the year this is comprehended in the sun's orbit.
The name Mithra, which the Gentiles use, gives the
same sum with different letters.[1]

Jerome's evidence is of much importance. He is the
only author apparently who assigns definite names to
the successive grades of Mithraic initiates. His ability
and scholarship enabled him better perhaps than most
of his contemporaries to understand and report on the
varieties of cult within the Roman Empire, and his
statement may be confidently accepted. The name
Heliodromus is apparently unique also in the literature.
The extract (a) is from *Ep.* CVII. *ad Lætam*, (b) and (c)
are from *Adv. Jovinianum* I. 7 and II. 14, (d) is from
Comm. in Amos, V. 9–10. Jerome (Eusebius Hierony-
mus) was born at Stridon in or about the year 346, and
died A.D. 420 at Bethlehem. It is worth notice also that
in connection with the grade of *miles*, soldier, reported
by Jerome Mithraism employs the term " sacramentum "
in the same manner as the Christian writers in relation
to the Christian rites of baptism, etc.

Eunapius : After himself there would arise a
priest to whom it was forbidden to sit upon the
priestly throne since it was consecrated to strange
divinities, and mighty oaths had he sworn not to take
part in strange rites. He declared nevertheless that he
would take part although not even an Athenian . . .
and his words came to pass in this way. For at the
same time that Agoræus [2] Vettius arose, founder of
the Mithraic cult, and for no long (period) . . . when a

---

[1] *I.e.* Μείθρας = 40 + 5 + 10 + 9 + 100 + 1 + 200 = 365;
Ἀβραξας = 1 + 2 + 100 + 1 + 60 + 1 + 200 = 365.
[2] The name is uncertain. Cumont prints (Ἀγόρ)ιος.

storm of misfortunes, numerous and indescribable,
had broken. . . .

Eunapius was a Greek philosopher and historian, born
at Sardis in 347 A.D. Educated at Athens he taught
rhetoric there in later life. He wrote brief " Lives of
Sophists," twenty-three in number, in a spirit hostile to
Christianity, and also a chronicle or history of events
from A.D. 270–404. The quotation above is from the
Life of Maximus, but the text is interrupted and obscure.

Prudentius : Kindly Guide, creator of the radiant
light, who controllest the seasons in their fixed
courses, if thy sun is hidden chaos grim encompasses
us, restore thy light O Christ to thy faithful followers.
  Though with countless stars thou hast adorned the
sky in all its grandeur, and with the splendour of
the moon, yet we go in quest of light from the cleft
rock, monstrous forms of stony birth.
  May men discern their hope of light enshrined in the
unchanging body of the Christ, who declared himself
to be the firm rock, whence our lesser fires have their
birth.

The words from Prudentius' Καθημερίνων (scil. ὕμνων)
V. are supposed to contain a reference to the tradition
of Mithra born from the rock. The association of
thought is not certain, and the language of Prudentius
is probably sufficiently explained by Matt. xvi. 18,
1 Cor. x. 4. The author was born in Spain 348 A.D.,
and his poems and hymns were held in great esteem,
some of the latter being used in the services of the
Christian Church. The *Cathemerinon,* as the name
implies, is a collection of lyrical poems for the days and
seasons.

Paul of Nola : What are we to say of their con-
cealment of the Invincible in a gloomy cavern, and
that to him whom they shroud in darkness they
venture to give the name of the sun ? He who in
secret offers homage to the light and hides in the
shades beneath the constellation of the sky, what is
he but the author of evil ?

Pontius Anicius Paulinus, 353–431 A.D., appointed
bishop of Nola in 409, whence his surname Nolanus,
was the author of poetical and other works, written both
before and after his conversion to Christianity. Of the
Christian poems most are dedicated to the memory of
Felix of Nola, martyr and saint. The passage quoted
is from the last of the thirty-six extant poems, and is
directed against the pagan faiths.

Augustine : (a) Some counterfeit therefore the
spirit of which I speak has set up, as though he would
fain redeem by blood his own image, since he knew
that by precious blood the human race was redeemed.
For evil spirits invent for themselves certain counterfeit representations of high degree, that by this
means they may deceive the followers of Christ.
To such an extent, my brethren, that these very
foes of ours, who delude by their posturings and
incantations and devices, mingle with their incantations the name of Christ. And because with poison
alone they are unable to lead the Christians astray,
they add a little honey, to conceal the bitter taste
by the sweet, that the fatal draught may be taken ;
to such an extent that as I understand at one time
the priest of that mitred god was accustomed to say,
" the mitred god himself [1] also was a Christian."

---

[1] *Ipse pileatus,* i.e. Mithra, but see Cumont's note.

(b) What travesty is it then that they enact in the cave with veiled faces? for they cover their eyes lest their deeds of shame should revolt them. Some like birds flap their wings imitating the raven's cry; others roar like lions; others bind their hands with the entrails of fowls and fling themselves down over pits full of water, and then another whom they call the Liberator approaches with a sword and severs the above-mentioned bonds. Other rites there are which are yet more dishonourable. What shameful mockeries for men who call themselves wise. But because these things are concealed in the darkness they think that they can remain unknown. Yet all these, the secret device and contrivance of foul and malignant demons, have been dragged to the light and unveiled by the holy Christian faith. For when the faith is preached the hearers of the excellent and sacred truth thus proclaimed have been converted, and have abandoned those dishonourable and secret rites, confessing that in their ignorance they have been misled.

Aurelius Augustinus, 354–430 A.D., was himself in early life a Manichæan and therefore acquainted from within with forms of heresy nearly related to Mithraism. He became bishop of Hippo *c.* 395 A.D. The *Quæstiones Veteris et Novi Testamenti*, from which the second extract is taken, is of doubtful authenticity, and has generally been supposed to be the work of Hilary the Deacon, about the middle of the fourth century. The reference of the first extract is less certain. It is from the *Tractatus in Joh. Evang.* VII. The " mitred god " has been supposed to be Mithra, who is so represented on the sculptures. In Cumont's judgement it is more

probable that Attis is meant, and that the reference here
is to the κριοβόλος, the sacrifice of the ram in his ritual.
The two faiths however were in close relation, and it is
likely that rites and customs were borrowed on both
sides.

> *Dionysius the Areopagite :* Accordingly of this the
> sacred records of the Persians make special mention,
> and to the present day the Magians celebrate the
> memorial rites of the triple Mithra.

The pseudepigraphic writings attributed to Dionysius
the Areopagite, the convert of St. Paul, Acts xvii. 34,
date probably from about the end of the fourth century.
The quotation is from the seventh of a collection of ten
letters, addressed to Polycarp. The reference is to a
miraculous lengthening of the day which is said to have
occurred in the time of Ezekiel.

> *Lampridius :* With his club he struck down not
> only the lions masquerading in woman's clothing
> and a lion's skin but even many men. Halt and
> lame men he dressed up as giants, so that covered
> with rags from the knees downwards they crept along
> like serpents, and transfixed them with arrows.
> The shrines of Mithra he defiled with human blood,
> judgeing that in this way he would terrorise by deed
> as well as by word.

Ælius Lampridius wrote biographies of several of the
Roman Emperors, one of which, that of Elagabalus, is
dedicated to Constantine. Part of his life therefore was
passed under the latter Emperor. Nothing more seems
to be known of him. The quotation is from the *Vita
Commodi*, ch. IX; and the words seem to refer to some
parody of the Mithraic rites, cp. *supra*, p. 50.

Claudian : Fragrant with clouds of incense and with sheaves of Sabæan corn the altars ensure peace. From the furthest shrines the priests draw forth the sacred flame and slay the bullocks with Chaldæan rite. The king himself with his right hand tips the gleaming bowl, and summons to witness Bel's mystic lore, and Mithra who guides the wandering stars.

At the end of the fourth and beginning of the fifth century Claudian was one of the greatest of the late Roman poets. He wrote numerous poems on historical, mythological and descriptive subjects, and a panegyric on Stilicho in three books, *De Consulatu Stilichonis, c.* 400 A.D., from which the above extract is taken, bk. I. 58 ff. A few letters also have been preserved.

Martian : The Latins call thee Sol, for that in solitary splendour thou art highest in rank after the Father, and from thy sacred head adorned with its twice six rays golden beams shoot forth, furnished thus, men say, to equal the number of the months and the seasons determined by thee. Four steeds they relate that thou guidest with reins, for thou alone dost control Nature's car. And for that thou expellest the darkness, disclosing the bright heavens with thy light, therefore they name thee Phœbus, revealer of the secrets of the future, or Lyæus because thou dost unloose the hidden things of night. Thee the Nile reveres as Serapis, Memphis as Osiris, other cults as Mithra, or Dis, or savage Typhon. Thou art fair Attis too, and the gentle boy of the curved plough, Ammon also of the parched Lybian desert, and Adon of Byblos. So under various names the whole world worships thee.

Martianus Capella wrote not earlier than the end of
the fourth century in prose and verse a work in nine
books on the liberal arts, to which he gave the strange
title of *De Nuptiis Philologiæ et Mercurii*. A native of
North Africa he practised rhetoric, apparently at
Carthage. The above invocation to the Sun is from
bk. II. 85.

Socrates : In the great city of Alexander a dis-
turbance arose from the following cause. There
was a district in the city, long waste and neglected,
a receptacle for stores of rubbish, wherein the
Greeks of old used to celebrate Mithraic rites and
perform human sacrifice. This vacant site Constantine had long previously assigned to the Alexandrian Church. Georgius however wishing to
build an oratory thereon gave orders for it to be
cleared. In the course of the work a shrine was
found at a considerable depth, in which were hidden
the mystical emblems of the Greeks; and these
comprised many human skulls, both ancient and new,
whose owners were reported to have been slain in
olden times, when the Greeks practised divination
by the entrails and offered magical sacrifices with
sorcery and deception. The Christians therefore
finding these in the shrine of Mithra hastened to turn
the mysteries of the Greeks to open ridicule before
all. They forthwith formed a procession and
exhibited the naked skulls to the populace. When
the Greeks of Alexandria saw this they were inflamed
with wrath, regarding it as an intolerable insult;
and availing themselves of any weapon to hand
they made an attack upon the Christians, and by
various means destroyed many of them. Some they

slew with swords, others were killed with clubs or
stones, and others strangled with cords; others
again they crucified, employing this manner of
death in mockery of the cross; and the greater
number they wounded. Then also as is the wont in
such circumstances they did not spare even their
nearest relatives, but friend smote friend, and
brother brother, and parents their children, and all
turned to mutual slaughter. The Christians therefore abandoned the cleansing of the Mithræum.
And others dragged Georgius from the church, bound
him to a camel and tore him asunder, and burned
both of them together. The king therefore indignant
at the murder of Georgius wrote a letter and up-
braided the people of Alexandria.

The *Ecclesiastical History* of Socrates in seven books
was written in the early part of the fifth century at
Constantinople, where the author's life was spent.
The history included the period from 306 to 439 A.D.
His title of Scholasticus was derived from his profession
as a lawyer. The extract is from bk. III. 2, 3.

Sozomen : The following event took place in connection with their so-called Mithræum. This place
which had long been waste was granted by Constantine to the Alexandrian church. When Georgius was
clearing it for the erection of a house of prayer a
shrine was disclosed, wherein were found some images
and the instruments of those who formerly practised
there initiatory and other rites. These were regarded
by those who saw them as ridiculous and bizarre;
and the Christians exhibited them publicly in procession in mockery of the Greeks. The latter

gathered a crowd together and set upon the Christians, arming themselves some with swords or stones,
others with any weapon to hand; and they slew
many, crucifying some by way of insult to their
religion, and inflicting wounds on most of them.
The Christians therefore left unfinished the work they
had begun; and the Greeks with the connivance of
the queen of Julian killed Georgius. The king himself moreover bears testimony to the truth of this.

The *Historia Ecclesiastica* of Sozomen for the greater
part relates to the same period as that of Socrates,
323 to 439 A.D., and he appears to have relied upon the
same source or sources. He was born about 400 A.D.
and dedicated his History in nine books to the Emperor
Theodosius II. By birth he is said to have been a
Christian of Palestine, and later to have studied and
practised in Constantinople. The passage quoted is
from bk. V. 7.

Proclus : (a) The barbarians call this life-giving
source the well of life,[1] the hollow receptacle suggest-
ing together with the quality of a well the virtue of
the whole life-giving godhead, wherein are contained
the springs of all life, divine, angelic, demoniac,
psychical, and physical.

If the one is spring-like (πηγαῖος), so also is the
other. What then are we to say? The barbarians
give to bowls the name of wells (πηγαίους), and so
they denote individual souls. This bowl therefore
is a bowl of living water (πηγαῖος κρατήρ); for it
is the source of souls, wherein souls. . . .

(b) They have natures therefore corresponding to

---

[1] πηγαίαν ψυχήν, a well-soul, living spring. There is an obscure
play upon words.

the majesty of their native gods. They worship
Aphrodite, whom they call Isis, and the son of
Kronos also . . . the sun they address as Mithra.
Most of them also foretell the future.

Proclus, the philosopher, surnamed Diadochus
(διάδοχος), successor *i.e.* of Plato, was born at Constantinople 412 A.D., and lived to the age of seventy-
three or seventy-four years. He studied philosophy
at Alexandria and Athens, and for many years taught
and shared in the public life of the latter city, being
renowned for the powers of his memory. Of his numerous works the commentaries on the writings of Plato
are the most important. The extracts (*a*) are from the
commentary on the Timæus, 315. D, F., and the barbarians referred to are supposed to be the followers of
Mithra; (*b*) is from a Paraphrase of the four books of
Ptolemy on the stellar influences, an elucidation of some
difficulties in Ptolemy's treatise.

Hesychius : Mithras, the name for the sun among
the Persians.
Mithres, the chief god among the Persians.

Cumont rightly explains the distinction made between
the two names as a mere confusion on the part of the
author of the Lexicon. Nothing is known of Hesychius,
or of his life. It is probable that he lived at the end of
the fourth or beginning of the fifth century, but by some
authorities he is placed earlier. His work is certainly
based upon the statements of earlier writers, grammarians
and lexicographers, and has been revised and amplified
by others at later dates.

The Armenian authors quoted are all attributed to
the fifth century of our era. Their information is not

to be considered as first-hand, but is probably derived from Greek sources.

> *Eznig de Goger :* (a) The Magi relate that when Ahriman saw that Ormuzd had created many things of beauty but had failed to bring forth the light he took counsel with the demons saying, " What good has Ormuzd secured? these his beautiful works remain shrouded in darkness, because he does not know how to make the light. Were he wise he might have a son Miher (the sun) by his mother, and the moon (Māh) by his sister." Then he commanded that this his counsel should not be disclosed. The demon Mahmi however when he had heard it betook himself immediately to Ormuzd and revealed the whole to him. " What folly ! you are clever enough to create the earth and the heavens and all that is in them, but unable to adopt common means like these."

> (b) The story runs that Ormuzd was invited by Ahriman to a feast. He came but only consented to eat on the condition that their sons were equally matched. The sons of Ahriman overthrew the sons of Ormuzd, and an arbiter was sought. Failing to find one however the two deities created the sun to discharge the office.

Esnik of Kolb, a village near Batoum on the Black Sea, is said to have taken part in the translation of the Bible into Armenian, and wrote a tract " Against the Sects," from which the above extracts are taken, probably about the middle of the fifth century. Nothing more seems to be known of him.

> *Agathangas :* St. Gregory made his way without delay to the district of Terdjan (in the province of

Erzerum), to make known there the religious teaching of the Apostles . . . he went also to the temple of
Mihr, the reputed son of Ormuzd, in the town which
the Parthians call Pakaiaridj,[1] and rased it to
the ground. The treasures he took and distributed
them to the poor, and consecrated the ground to the
Church, confirming the inhabitants in the knowledge
of the truth.

Agathangas, or Agathangelus according to the
tradition, was secretary to the king Tiridates II, and
wrote a history of his reign, from which (ch. X) the above
notice is derived. The history is far from being a sober
narrative of facts, and it is improbable that the tradition
as to the author's position and office is correct. Cumont
believes him to have been an Armenian priest of the
middle of the fifth century.

Elisæus Vartabad : (a) You have said that God
was born of a woman ; that should not arouse in you
repulsion or scorn. Ormuzd also and Ahriman were
born of a father, but not of a mother. If you reject
the one statement you cannot maintain the other.
It is however a most strange thing, that the god
Mihr should be born of a woman.

(b) One of your most ancient sages has declared
that the god Mihr was born of a human mother. He
is none the less king, son of God, and noble kin of the
seven gods.

(c) The gods are benevolent and regardful of the
human race, if only men acknowledge the greatness

---

[1] In the Greek rendering the name is given as Βαγαυρίζ. It
seems impossible to determine what place, if any, was intended.
The same Greek translator names Hephaestus as the deity whose
temple was destroyed, apparently identifying Mithra with
Hephaestus, as others also appear to have done.

of the gods and their own insignificance, and take
pleasure in the gifts of the earth distributed by the
hands of the king, from whose lips proceed the decrees
of life and of death. Their will is supreme, and the
sun also should be worshipped, for his rays illuminate
the whole world, and his warmth sustains man and
beast. His bounty is bestowed without partiality
on all,[1] and men name him therefore the Divine
Mihr, for in him there is neither guile nor ignorance.

(d) The chief executioner replied : I swear by the
god Mihr that you speak more rashly than your
instructors. You are evidently yet more guilty. It
is therefore impossible to shield you from death
unless you worship the sun and comply with the
demands of our religion.

Elisæus, the writer, and historian of the war which the
Armenians waged on behalf of their faith against the
persecuting king Yezdegird II, 449–451 A.D., is usually
identified with a bishop of the same name who took part
in a Synod at Artashat (Artaxata) in the year 449.
The vizier of the Persian king bore the name of Mihr-
Nerseh, and the extracts (a) and (b) are from an apology
addressed to him by Armenian bishops. The third
quotation gives the words of a Persian official to the
Christians, the fourth and last invokes the authority of
Mithra for the sentence against the Christian Martyrs.

Zosimus : (a) Dry the substance then in the sun
and preserve it as a mystery not to be revealed,
which none of the sages ventured to communicate by
word but only by signs. For it is an indication of
this that in their esoteric writings they use the word

---

[1] Cp. Matt. v. 45.

stone for that which is not a stone, the unknown
they describe as universally known, the dishonoured
as highly honoured, the ungenerous as divinely
bountiful. Let me then also extol heaven's real
gift, which alone in our daily experience rises above
the material; for this is the medicine that is potent
to heal, the Mithraic mystery.

(b) Aurelian . . . after the capture and destruction of
Palmyra . . . celebrated a triumph at Rome, and was
received with the utmost enthusiasm by the Senate
and people. He built the temple of the Sun also on
a magnificent scale, adorning it with the votive
offerings from Palmyra, and set up statues of the
Sun and Bel.

Zosimus, the Greek historian, flourished in the middle
or end of the fifth century. There was also a pope of
that name who occupied the Roman see from March to
December in the year 417 A.D. It is improbable that
either of these was the author of the collection of magical
charms or prescriptions from which the above extract
(a) is taken. In the text the words are repeated
τὸν ἀδώρητον καὶ θεοδώρητον, but it seems impossible to
reproduce the verbal play or jugglery in English, if
indeed the repetition is real and not a mere copyist's
error. The second quotation is from the *Historia Nova*
I. 61, but the supposed reference to Mithra is doubtful.

Nonnus of Panopolis : (a) Turn if thou will thy
steps to the near country of the Medes ; thither go and
address the chorus bands of Dionysus. I will show
thee the land of Bactria, where the divine Mithra
had his birth, the Assyrian lord of light in Persis.
For Deriades [1] never learnt to know the race of the

---

[1] Deriades was the Indian king.

F

blessed gods of heaven, nor does honour to the Sun
or Zeus or the chorus band of the bright stars. . . . I
take no heed of the blessed offspring of Zeus; for the
twain Earth and Water alone have become my gods.

(b) With revelry he approached the home of
Astrochiton [1] and the leader of the stars, and in
mystic tones uttered his invocation : Herakles star-
adorned, king of fire, ruler of the universe, thou sun,
who with thy far-flung rays art the guardian of
mortal life, with flashing beam [2] revolving the wide
circuit of thy course . . . Belus thou art named on the
Euphrates, Ammon in Libya, Apis of the Nile art
thou by birth, Arabian Kronos, Assyrian Zeus . . .
but whether thou art Sarapis, or the cloudless Zeus
of Egypt, or Kronos, or Phaethon, or many-titled
Mithra, Sun of Babylon, or in Greece Apollo of Delphi,
or Wedlock, whom Love begat in the shadowy land
of dreams . . . whether thou art known as Paieon, the
healer of pain, or Æther with its varied garb, or
star-bespangled Night—for the starry robes of night
illuminate the heaven—lend a propitious ear to my
prayer.

Nonnus, the author of a Greek epic poem in forty-
eight books, was a native of Panopolis in Egypt. Except
that he was a Christian, and lived at the end of the
fourth or beginning of the fifth century, nothing seems
to be known of his life. The theme of his poem the
Dionysiaca (Διονυσιακά) is Dionysus, but it ranges over
a wide mythological field, and contains little or nothing
to suggest a Christian origin. Nonnus is credited also
with the authorship of a paraphrase of St. John's Gospel

---

[1] Star-bespangled, star-adorned, the epithet of Herakles.
[2] δίσκῳ, read probably δ'φρῳ, " with thy gleaming car."

in hexameters. The passages quoted are from *Dionys.*
XXI. 246 ff., and XL. 365 ff.

> *John Lydus :* The western region being assigned
> to the element earth it was natural for the Romans
> to take the latter under their care. For this reason
> they appear to have honoured Vesta above all, as
> the Persians the rock-born Mithra because of the
> region of fire, and the dwellers in the north the watery
> element because of the region of water, and the
> Egyptians Isis, meaning the moon,[1] the guardian
> of the entire atmosphere.

John Lydus, Ἰωάννης Λαυρέντιος, was born at Phila-
delphia, in Lydia, in the year 490 A.D., whence his
surname of the Lydian. He studied philosophy at
Constantinople, and became private secretary or
amanuensis to the Roman prefect, from whom he is
said to have received marks of distinction and considerable sums of money. Later in life he devoted
himself to literature, and wrote poems, none of which
have been preserved. His work, Περὶ Μηνῶν Συγγραφή,
or *De Mensibus*, from which the above extract is taken,
III. 26, is a historical account of the Roman festivals
based on older authorities, two epitomes of which only
are extant.

> *Damascius :* Epiphanius and Euprepius were both
> Alexandrians by birth, with a profound knowledge of
> the religious observances there practised. Euprepius
> presided over the so-called Persian rites, Epiphanius

---

[1] διὰ τὴν σελήνην, " on account of the moon," but omit διά, or
read perhaps διὰ τὸ κέντρον τῆς σελήνης, because of the region
of the moon, lit. " point " or " centre." Isis was identified with
the moon.

over those in which Osiris was honoured, and further
over those of the god celebrated as the Eternal, of
whom I might write, but for the present at least I
abstain. Of these rites also however Epiphanius
was in charge.

Damascius is a title, of Damascus, and the real name
of the author and philosopher who bore the title is
unknown. He was born about the end of the fifth
century, and studied and taught Neo-Platonism at
Alexandria and Athens. His chief works were commentaries on Plato and Aristotle. The above extract
however is from Suidas, *Lexicon*, I. 2, who attributes
it to "Damascius." The "Persian rites" are those of
Mithra, and these therefore in the writer's time were
known and practised at Alexandria.

Cosmas Indicopleustes : It is reported that to the
present time the Persians keep the festival of Mithra,
that is of the sun, in memory of the miracle of the
time of Ezekiel.

See above, Dionysius the Areopagite, p. 66. Cosmas,
surnamed Indicopleustes from his travels, of which he
has left a most interesting record, was a native of Egypt,
and spent his early life in Alexandria. He is said to have
studied under Theodore of Mopsuestia, and in later life
to have become a monk. His narrative was written
c. 550 A.D. ; the passage quoted will be found in 165 A.

Maximus the Confessor : To this the Persians bear
testimony, when they give to the sun the name of
Mithra, and thus by their celebration of the memorial
rites of the "threefold" recall the lengthening of
that day.

The allusion is to the tradition that in the time of Ezekiel the day was prolonged to threefold its usual length, see above, p. 66, Dionysius the Aeropagite.

Maximus, c. 580 to 662 A.D., known as Confessor and Martyr, wrote extensively in the early part of the seventh century in defence of the orthodox Christian faith against the Monothelite heresy. He became abbot of a monastery at Scutari in 639, and seems to have travelled in Greece and Egypt, suffering persecution in later life and dying in banishment. The note above is from a scholion attributed to him.

Nonnus, the Mythographer : (*a*) Mithra therefore the Persians consider to be the sun, do sacrifice to him, and observe certain rites in his honour. No one can participate in his service without passing first through the grades of discipline. These grades are eighty in number, with descent and ascent, for the tests applied are first of an easier character, then more difficult ; and thus after passing through all the grades the disciple arrives at perfection. The successive disciplinary tests are by fire, by cold, by hunger and thirst, by prolonged exertion, and in a word by similar trials of all kinds.

(*b*) Mithra is considered by the Persians to be the sun. And to him they offer many sacrifices, and observe certain rites in his honour. No one can be initiated into the rites of Mithra without passing through all the disciplines and giving proof of self-control and chastity. Eighty grades are enumerated through which the postulant must pass in succession ; for example, plunging first into deep water for many days, then throwing himself into fire, then solitary fasting in a desert place, and others also until as

stated above he has passed through the eighty.   Then
finally if he survives he receives the highest initiation,
or if he has succumbed an (honourable) sepulture.[1]

(c) Different views are held with regard to Mithra.
Some identify him with the sun, others with the
guardian of the fire, others with a specific force,
and certain rites are observed in his honour, especially
among the Chaldæans.   The aspirants to initiation
pass through a series of disciplinary grades, under-
going first the easier forms of penance, then the
more difficult.   For example fasting is first imposed
upon the neophytes for a period of about fifty days.
If this is successfully endured, for two days they are
exposed to extreme heat,[2] then again plunged into
snow for twenty days.   And thus the severity of the
discipline is gradually increased, and if the postulant
shows himself capable of endurance he is finally
admitted to the highest grades.

Nonnus, whose title is by way of distinction from others
of the same name, wrote a commentary or scholia on
the work of Gregory Nazianzen, *In Julianum Impera-
torem invectivæ duæ*, from which the first two extracts
above are derived.   His date is uncertain, but he is said
to have lived in Palestine in the middle of the sixth
century;   more probably a century later.   The third
quotation is from the commentary on *In sancta lumina*,
cp. *supra*, p. 58.

Theophylact Simokattes : (a) Gazing up into heaven
and acknowledging the creator, disowning the false
gods and placing no hope in Mithra, he averted the

---

[1] The meaning of the last phrase is not quite certain.   The
text is perhaps imperfect.

[2] ξυσθῆναι, *v.l.* ξεσθῆναι.   Read ζεσθῆναι.

imminent peril, changing faith and fortune to brighter issues.

(b) For lions are subdued, dragons are muzzled, Bel and Mithra are put in fetters.

Theophylact Simokata (Σιμοκάτης), an Egyptian by birth, wrote a history of the wars of the emperor Maurice A.D. 582–602. Other works of his on scientific and literary subjects have been preserved. The reference in the first passage, *Hist.* IV. 10, is to the Persian king Chosroes II, who after his defeat in A.D. 590 is represented as rejecting the false gods that have betrayed him to his ruin. The words of the second extract, *Hist.* IV. 16, are descriptive of the Divine power.

Cosmas of Jerusalem is the source of the third extract from Nonnus, (c) *supra*, p. 80, and he further adds :

The disciplinary grades of Mithra are reported to be eighty in number, through which the candidate for initiation must pass in succession. In addition to those already described there is immersion in water for many days, passing through fire, solitude and fasting in the wilderness, and numerous others until the end of the eighty disciplines is reached. And they do not allow participation in the rites of Mithra to anyone who has not passed through all the grades and approved himself pure and self-controlled.

Cosmas, known as Cosmas the younger, was a native of Jerusalem, and became bishop of Maiuma in Palestine in 743 A.D. To him are attributed many hymns and other poetical compositions, some of which are found

in the service books of the Greek Church at the present
day.

Moses of Khorene : We swear by the great god
Mihr that we will not do any harm to thy royal
throne.

Late in the fifth century, Moses of Khorene, perhaps
the most widely known and renowned of Armenian
historians, wrote a history of Armenia in three parts
from the earliest period to the fall of the Arsacid dynasty
in 428 A.D. At a later date the work was either rewritten
or freely interpolated, for references and names are
introduced which belong to a period after the death of
the author. This recension is to be dated in the seventh
or eighth century. The passage quoted, I. 2. 17, is from
a letter of the Persian king Sapor to the king of Armenia.

Theophanes : In this year Galerius Maximianus
was persuaded by a sorcerer Theoteknos to sacrifice
to the demons and to receive oracles. Theoteknos
entered a cave and delivered to him an oracle against
the Christians in order to arouse persecution.

Cumont argues that inasmuch as Galerius was an
adherent of Mithraism the priest referred to must have
been a priest of that religion. Theophanes, a Christian
abbot in the second half of the seventh century, wrote
a chronicle of events from the accession of the Emperor
Diocletian, 277 A.D., to the year 811, four or five years
before his own death in banishment in Samothrace.
The chronicle is arranged according to years *anno mundi*,
of which the extract as given by Cumont is 5794.

Suidas : The Persians regard Mithra as the sun,
and offer many sacrifices to him. No one however

can be initiated into his service without passing through certain disciplinary grades and approving himself pure and steadfast.

Nothing is certainly known either of the date or author of the *Lexicon* that passes under the name of Suidas. The nucleus may have been composed as early as the ninth or tenth century, the writer availing himself of ancient authorities. Large additions and interpolations were made subsequently, the limits of which cannot now be assigned. The extract is from Vol. II. p. 847, *s.v.* Μίθρου.

INDEX

A

'Abodā Zārā, 23
Abraxas, 61, and note
Agathangas, 72 f.
Ahriman, 72 f.
Ahuramazda, 5, 13, 20
Alexander, Alexandria, 27, 53 f., 68 f., 71, 78
Amshaspands, 29 n.
Anubis, 40
Aphrodite, 24 f., 45, 47, 49, 71
Apollo, 47, 60, 76
Armenian, 71 f., 74, 82
Arnobius, 52 f.
Aryan deities, 5 f.
Asia Minor, 7, 10
Athenæus of Naucratis, 25 f.
Athene, 55
Athens, 58, 60 f., 63, 71, 78
Attis, 40, 66 f.
Aurelian, 75
Avesta, 19 ff.

B

Babylon, Babylonia, 13, 76
Bactria, 75
bees, 48
Bel, Belus, 75 f., 81
Boghaz Keui, 5
Buddha, 14
bull, in Mithraism, 13 ff., 23 f., 37 f., 48 f., 52

C

Celsus, 45 ff.
Chaldæan, 57, 59, 80

Christianity, relation to Mithraism, vi, 1 f., 4, 16 f., and passim.
Claudian, 67
Clement, 47
Commodian, 51
Comparative Religion, vi.
Constantine, 66
Cosmas Indicopleustes, 78
Cosmas of Jerusalem, 81
Cumont, F., v, 17 f., and passim.
Cyrus, 25

D

Damascius, 77 f.
Daniel, 40
Darius, 28, 50, 53 f.
Demeter, 48
Deucalion, 35
Dieterich, A., v
Diocletian, 82
Dion Cassius, 44
Dion Chrysostom, 31
Dionysius the Areopagite, 66, 78 f.
Dionysus, 75
discipline, grades of, 79 ff., 83
Duris, 26

E

Eleusis, 60
Elisæus Vartabad, 73 f.
Epiphanius, 40, 77 f.
Eubulus, 50, 61
Eunapius, 62 f.

85

Printed in Great Britain by
Richard Clay & Sons, Limited,
Bungay, Suffolk.